You Can Be a Professional Photographer

Arthur Liebers

You Can Be a Professional Photographer

Illustrated with photographs

Vocations in Trades

Lothrop, Lee & Shepard Books · New York

Vocations in Trades books by Arthur Liebers

YOU CAN BE A CARPENTER

YOU CAN BE AN ELECTRICIAN

YOU CAN BE A MACHINIST

YOU CAN BE A MECHANIC

YOU CAN BE A PLUMBER

YOU CAN BE A PRINTER

YOU CAN BE A PROFESSIONAL DRIVER

YOU CAN BE A WELDER

Exploring Careers book by Arthur Liebers

JOBS IN CONSTRUCTION

Title-page photograph courtesy of Fashion Institute of Technology.

 Inquiries should be addressed to Lothrop, Lee & Shepard Books, a division of William Morrow & Company, Inc., 105 Madison Ave., New York, N. Y. 10016.
Printed in the United States of America.
1 2 3 4 5 6 7 8 9 10

A *Vocations in Trades* book

Library of Congress Cataloging in Publication Data
Liebers, Arthur, (date)
You can be a professional photographer.
(His Vocations in trades)
Bibliography: p.
Includes index.
SUMMARY: Discusses the education and preparation needed for a career in photography and how to get information about jobs in such areas as portrait, fashion, news, industrial, medical, and undersea photography.
1. Photography—Vocational guidance—Juvenile literature. [1. Photography—Vocational guidance. 2. Vocational guidance] I. Title.
TR154.L53 770′.232 79-12484
ISBN 0-688-41890-2
ISBN 0-688-51890-7 lib. bdg.

Acknowledgments

This book could not have been written without the cooperation of the photographic industry and so many persons involved in the world of the camera.

The Eastman Kodak Company's Educational Division was always on hand with useful information. The Professional Photographers' Association and its publication *The Professional Photographer* presented the views of those working in the field. Elaine Kay Willenson of the Germain School of Photography was most helpful in providing material on photographic study curricula. Where not otherwise indicated, course descriptions were provided by the Germain School.

In previous books, the author has expressed thanks to Anna Urband of the U.S. Navy's Media Service; again she responded to every call for assistance.

Virginia Croft Lopez of VICA provided information on photography activities in the Vocational Industrial Clubs of America.

The Rochester Institute of Technology was most cooperative in providing data on the scientific aspects of photography, as was the Biological Photographic Association.

The Occupational Outlook Handbook of the U.S. Department of Labor was a valuable source of Information.

Other credits appear in the text and in captions for the photographs.

Special thanks are due to Stan Young, professional photographer of Remsenburg, N.Y., for his many suggestions.

El Winesburg of the Tulsa County (Oklahoma) Area Vocational-Technical School provided information on the VICA program in photography and photographs of VICA participants.

Information on photographers' assistants is excerpted with permission from "Want to Break Into the Business? Be a Photographer's Assistant" by Richard Busch, a Chronicle Guidance Publications, Inc., reprint, which originally appeared in *Popular Photography* magazine.

Contents

(*Courtesy of The New York Historical Society*)

In this wagon, G. W. Pach drove around summer resorts looking for customers who wanted their pictures taken. This photograph was taken around 1876 at Ocean Grove, New Jersey.

1/Photography As a Career

Is Photography the Right Career for You?

This is a book about photography, but it is not a book that will teach you how to take pictures. The whole idea behind this book is to give you an idea of the many different ways to make a career for yourself by using a camera. To help you decide whether photography is the right career for you, we will try to describe the varied work done by photographers, and show how you can prepare yourself for this interesting vocation.

As a rule, most photographers specialize in some particular type of photography. Sometimes it is just because that happens to be the type of work they are able to get. Sometimes it is because they feel they have a special talent or desire for that kind of work. A good photographer must have a "feel" for recognizing a potentially good photograph and a talent for composing the subjects of photographs, something like a painter's talent in laying out a painting or sketch.

Photographers use their cameras and film to catch an image of people, places, and events much as a writer uses words. Those with talent and the eye for it can capture the personality of individuals or the mood of scenes which they photograph. Photographers with other skills specialize in scientific, medical, or engineering photography.

2/Kinds of Photographers

Portrait Photographers

Portrait work provides a career for many photographers. Portrait photographers take pictures of individuals or groups of persons. Perhaps you have had your picture taken by a portrait photographer for your school yearbook. This kind of work is usually done in the photographer's studio, but for special events such as weddings, photographs are taken in churches or temples and homes.

Opportunities for portrait photographers can be found everywhere. In the smallest towns and in the largest cities, there will be many listings in the yellow pages of the phone book under "Photographers-Portrait."

(Courtesy of The New York Historical Society)

The skylight room of a photographer's gallery in 1857. The subject could not move for minutes while the photograph was being taken.

(Courtesy of The New York Historical Society)

This photograph, taken on July 4, 1862, shows the wagon of Matthew Brady, the famous Civil War photographer. He used such wagons to develop and print his pictures.

In smaller studios, the portrait photographer handles all operations. He schedules his work, sets up equipment, and takes the pictures. Then he (or she) develops and retouches the negatives, prepares proofs, and mounts and frames pictures. In addition, the photographer must be a good business person. Payments have to be collected, records kept, and bills paid.

Commercial Photographers

Commercial photographers photograph a wide range of subjects including manufactured articles, buildings, livestock, and large groups of people. They frequently take photographs for catalogs. Those in advertising take pictures to promote such items as clothing, furniture, automobiles, and food, and may specialize in one such area. Advertising photographers must know how to use many different photographic techniques.

Industrial Photographers

The work of industrial photographers may appear in company publications that report to stockholders or advertise company products or services, and in "house organs"—company publications distributed to employees. The photographs usually show workers on the job or at company functions, or operating any new machinery or equipment. Industrial photographers also take motion pictures of workers operating machinery and equipment.

Many industrial photographers work on research projects. Medical researchers often use ultraviolet and infrared photography, fluorescence and X-rays to obtain photographs that could not be taken under normal light. Time lapse photography (see Glossary), photomicrography (where the subject of the photograph may be magnified fifty or seventy times or more), and photogrammetry (surveying an area by aerial photography) are other special techniques.

Other photographic specialties include photojournalism, or press photography, which requires a "nose for news" combined with photographic ability.

You probably know the term "Audiovisual" as applied to educational materials. It means teaching materials that use pictures and often sound equipment in the classroom or for individual teaching. In this field, photographers help educators in preparing this material. Photographs taken by the

(Courtesy of "Professional Photographer" magazine)

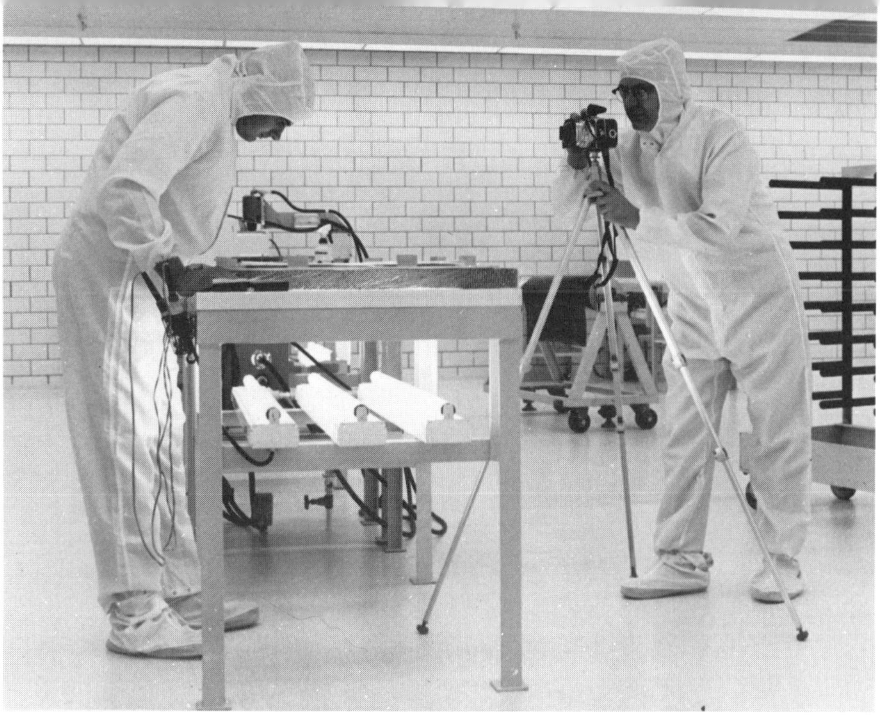

This *clean room* in an industrial plant has to be almost as sterile as a hospital operating room. The photographer, on the right, has to dress accordingly.

Press photographers at the scene of a multiple murder and suicide at a North Carolina shopping center.

(UPI photo)

educational photographer appear in books and magazines, on slides and in filmstrips, and sometimes on motion picture film or TV tapes. Equipment of this type is used in schools and for adult education.

The Photographer's Tools

Although, as you have seen, their subject matter varies, all photographers use the same basic equipment. The most important item, of course, is the camera, and most photographers own several.

Unlike snapshot cameras, which have a lens permanently attached to the camera body, most professional cameras are constructed to use a variety of lenses designed for close-up, medium range, or distance photography, or for desired special effects.

In addition to more complex cameras, professional photographers need a variety of other equipment in their work. They should be able to use different kinds of film and colored filters to obtain desired effects under different lighting conditions. When taking pictures after dark or indoors, they must be able to use electric flash units, floodlights, and other special lighting equipment.

Various kinds of tripods and camera stands, extra lenses, strobe lights, wires, cable releases, film, clamps, tape, black and white cardboard, envelopes for film, all kinds of repair tools, must be on hand when needed. Usually all this material is handled by the photographer's assistant, who is responsible for double-checking that anything the photographer needs when he or she begins shoot-

(NASA photo)

An Apollo 12 astronaut on the moon. The astronaut taking his picture is reflected in his face shield.

Practicing their photography techniques before setting off on a trip to the moon, these astronauts prepare to photograph a mockup of the Surveyor Spacecraft at the Kennedy Space Center.

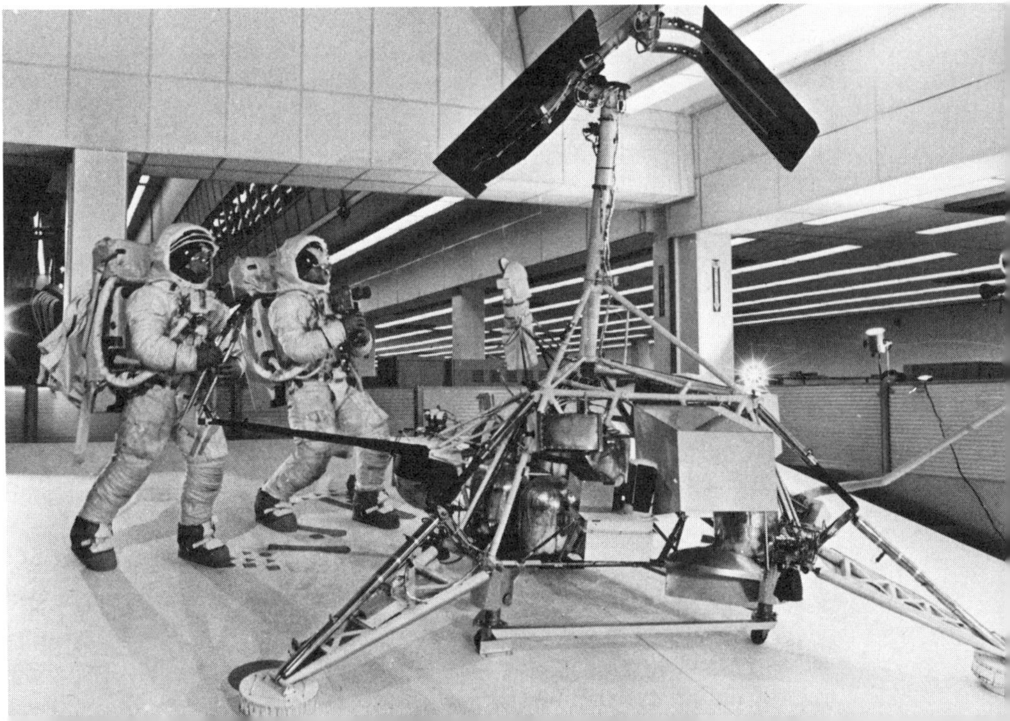

(NASA photo)

ing is available. You will find more about the assistant's role in professional photography on pages 26 to 31.

Some photographers develop and print their own photographs in the darkroom and may enlarge or otherwise alter the basic image. Others send their work to photographic laboratories for processing.

Because the procedures involved in still photography are quite different from those in motion picture work, photographers usually specialize in one or the other. Also, many work in TV studios or outside with the portable mini-cam TV cameras and sound equipment. However, there is growing demand for photographers who have training in both types of photography.

This motion picture cameraman works for the Tennessee Valley Authority.

(Tennessee Valley Authority photo)

Where Do Photographers Work?

The United States Government recently studied the photographic business. The investigators found that more than 85,000 persons are working photographers. Most are employed in commercial studios. The next largest number work for newspapers and magazines. Other large-scale employers of photographers are government agencies, photographic equipment suppliers and dealers, and industrial firms. Some photographers teach in colleges and universities, and some in the motion picture and television fields.

About 30,000 men and women work on their own as free-lance photographers, selling their work to advertisers, magazines, and newspapers.

Here are only a few of the possible specialties of free-lance photographers:

- Photographs of babies and children
- Feature and news photos for local papers
- Pet portraits
- Advertising postcards and brochures
- Photos for local company publications
- Photos for newspaper advertisements
- Real estate photographs for local realtors
- Preparing photo-albums for weddings, Bar-Mitzvahs, other events
- Photos of new store exteriors
- Photos of private homes
- Photos of boats for their owners
- Aerial photographs

One practical reason for choosing photography as your future career is that jobs are found in al-

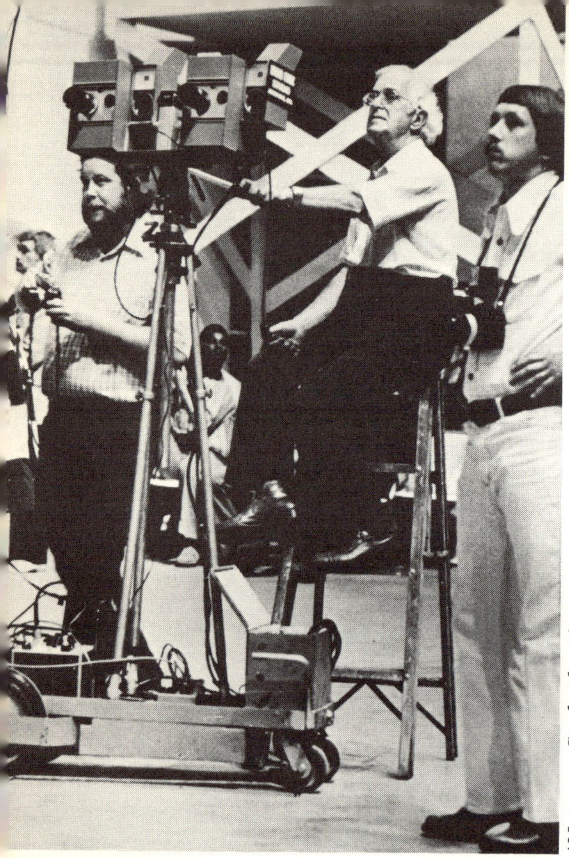

(Norman Cook photo)

Many photographers become specialists in some field. Norman Cook of Anderson, Indiana, has been a professional photographer for over 50 years. He designed a camera system for taking class graduating pictures that can take and identify entire graduating classes in uninterrupted sequence. He has what is believed to be the world record of 1,640 pictures in one hour. Here you see him, with two assistants, preparing to photograph a college graduating class.

most every part of the country. News photographers may be sent overseas on special projects, and photographers for travel magazines go all over the world. So whether you have a yen for travel or prefer to live in a big city or settle in a small community, a career in photography can offer you a choice.

Education in Photography

As in other fields, the better prepared you are, the farther you can go.

In the United States there are almost 700 different kinds of schools in which you can study photography. Among these are colleges, universities, community and junior colleges, art schools, and schools that teach only photography.

If your goal is to learn the basics of photography and then get into the field, many local community

(McGraw-Hill Publications photo)

For McGraw-Hill architectural magazines and books, the director of photography takes a picture of an architecture student at the University of Mexico. Some trade-publication photographers go all over the world.

or junior colleges have two-year programs leading to a certificate or an associate degree in photography. In every state there are numerous schools which specialize in teaching photography. There are also correspondence schools which offer courses in different kinds of photography. However, before signing up for one of these schools, have someone like your school counselor or librarian check up on the credentials and reputation of the school.

Four years of college, with a major or main goal in photography, will prepare you for many of the better-paying positions.

A number of universities have courses in research in such fields as developing new photographic equipment or methods, leading to a master's degree.

A few universities offer Ph.D. programs in photography, where you can graduate with the title of "doctor" and have an opportunity to qualify for college-level teaching or advanced research.

Professionals in the field say that a formal education in photography gives a solid, fundamental background in equipment, processes, and techniques. Art schools offer valuable training in design and composition, but not the technical training needed for professional photographic work.

The armed forces also train many young people in photographic skills. (For more about that see pages 93 to 99.)

There are no set educational requirements for becoming a photographer, but you should have at least a high school education. Some of the instruction manuals and equipment that the photographer must understand are fairly complicated, and often a photographer must write a caption for the picture he has taken, and this should be done in correct English.

Many high schools have courses in photography, and some high schools have camera clubs. In many areas BOCES (Bureau of Cooperative Educational Services) programs offer training in using cameras and in darkroom work.

You Can Learn by Doing

Some people prepare for work as a photographer in a commercial studio through two or three years of on-the-job training as a photographer's

One problem of the commercial photographer is to get the most out of any subject he photographs. Here, a student is trying to figure out a way to glamorize a picture of four cans.

(Ferris State College photo)

assistant. Usually studios prefer trainees who are high school graduates. You generally start in the darkroom where you learn the techniques of mixing chemicals, developing film, photoprinting, and enlarging. Later you may set up lights and cameras or help an experienced photographer take pictures.

Scientific Photography

Amateur experience in taking photographs coupled with a desire to learn may be enough to get a starting job as a photographer's assistant, but more advanced education is usually needed for industrial or scientific photography. To be successful in these specialties you must be more than just a competent photographer: you should have some knowledge of the field in which the photography is used. For example, work in scientific, medical, or engineering research requires a background in the particular science or engineering specialty as well as skill in photography.

Do You Have These Traits?

For success in photography, you should have good eyesight and color vision. Manual dexterity—the ability to use your hands well—is essential in working with photographic equipment.

In addition, you should be patient and should enjoy working with detail. In your educational background you will need some knowledge of mathematics, physics, and chemistry to understand the use of various lenses, films, light sources, and development processes.

Some of the photographic fields require additional qualities. Advertising and other business photographers must be imaginative and original

Off the Antarctic Peninsula, a scuba diver prepares to photograph marine flora and fauna for a study of intertidal algae and invertebrates at Oregon State University.

(U.S. Navy photo)

in their thinking. News photographers must be able to recognize a good photo possibility and act quickly. Otherwise, an opportunity to capture an important event on film may be lost.

Photographers who specialize in portrait photography need the ability to help their subjects relax in front of the camera.

Career Advancement

Newly hired photographers are usually given relatively routine assignments that do not require split-second camera adjustments or decisions on what subject matter to photograph. News photographers, for example, may be assigned to cover local meetings or photograph snowstorms. After gaining experience they may advance to more demanding assignments, and some may move to staff positions on national news magazines or large newspapers.

Photographers with exceptional ability may gain national recognition and have their work exhibited in galleries or published in books.

Some industrial or scientific photographers may be appointed to supervisory positions. Magazine and news photographers may become heads of graphic arts departments or photography editors.

What Are Your Prospects in Photography?

One thing you should ask yourself in planning your career is: What are my chances of making a good living in that kind of work?

Getting into the photographic field has never been easy. One problem is that almost anyone with a camera can say, "I am a photographer." However, without some talent and preparation for the work, a beginner won't last very long.

Today, the most promising field to try for is in business and industry. More and more photographs are being used in presentations at meetings, stockholders' reports, sales campaigns, and public relations work. Photography is also becoming an increasingly important part of law enforcement work. In scientific and medical research, there will be opportunities for those with the needed background.

In the fields of commercial, or business, and portrait photography, it is expected that there will be slow growth in the 1980s, and competition for jobs as photographers' assistants will be keen. These two fields are relatively crowded, since photographers can go into business for themselves with a fairly small financial investment, or work part-time while holding another job. The increasing use of self-processing cameras (such as the Polaroids) in commercial photography has contributed to the crowding in this field, because little photographic training is required for their use.

To Become a Professional

Most amateur photographers never take the plunge into the photography business, writing off the idea of professional photography as wishful thinking, as something too far beyond them to consider seriously. But others either make their way to the big cities to give it a try or do so in their home communities.

Be a Photographer's Assistant

By the thousands, they knock on photographers' doors every year looking for the opportunity to earn meager wages ($125 a week on the average) to perform all kinds of routine, mostly manual tasks—building sets, loading cameras and film holders, mixing chemicals, developing film and making prints, setting up lights, scouting locations, sweeping floors, dusting, painting, ordering supplies, lugging boxes of equipment, loading station wagons or vans, going for coffee, and countless other tasks—in exchange for the privilege of being on the professional scene and having the opportunity to learn the craft directly from a skilled and experienced professional.

Then, after some months or years (usually years) of being an integral part of the studio operation, participating closely in hundreds of actual shooting assignments, and really coming to understand how to solve the endless problems that confront photographers in all kinds of situations, many of these assistants finally leave the nest and venture forth on their own to become professionals.

The Best Way to Break in

Many photographers and assistants agree that this is by far the best way to break into the field, much more valuable than what can be learned in even the best schools that teach photography. "You can learn many of the techniques in a good photography course," says Gideon Lewin, who graduated from the well-regarded Los Angeles Art Center College of Design's photo department, and has been assisting the noted photographer Richard Avedon for eleven years, "but they don't give you a very realistic view of what it is like to work in a professional studio.

"Even though schools give assignments to simulate true situations, they are never the same as the real thing; when you're getting paid for it, when you have the responsibility for a five-thousand-dollar job, when you have to deliver with a perfect job, when there is no excuse."

But this does not mean that schooling is unimportant. In fact, most knowledgeable people in the field agree that school is the best place of all to acquire the kind of solid fundamental background in hardware, film processing, lighting and basic technique that is so important to have when looking for a good assistant's job. Many top photographers will not even consider hiring someone who has not already studied in a good school.

What Will You Learn?

The experience gained by an assistant can vary greatly from one studio to the next. Some photographers are relaxed and willing to take the assistant

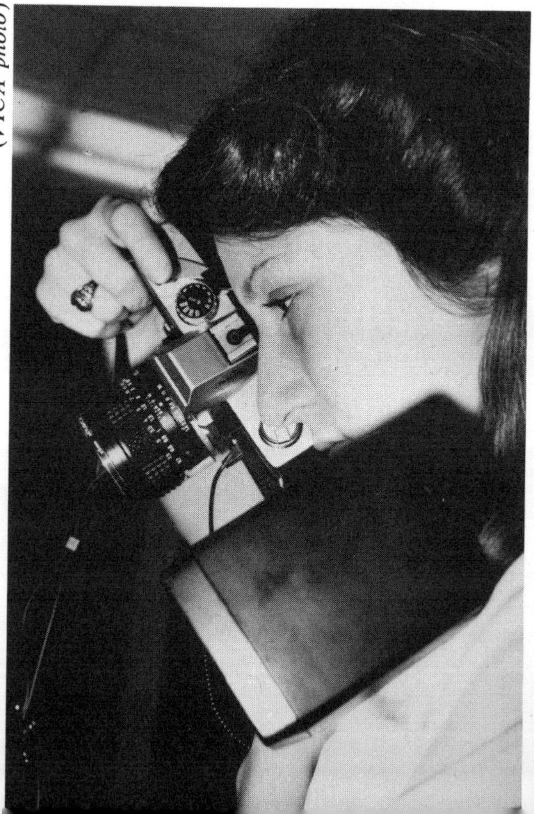

(*VICA photo*)

This student is learning to handle a fairly complex professional-type camera. She's using a 35mm Single Lens Reflex camera.

(Alan Perlman photo for Nikon)

Norman Snyder, editor of a photography catalog, is shown using a Nikon camera with a 1000mm lens. A compact Nikon camera hangs from his neck.

under their wing, explaining techniques and approaches as they work together. Many such photographers will allow their assistants to be in on all aspects of the business, including meetings with clients, and often give them the freedom to construct sets, light them, and even take the picture, entirely on their own. Other photographers may be less generous and trusting, treating their assistants as mere flunkies, allowing them little freedom and responsibility, jealously hiding secrets, and remaining generally disinterested in the master-apprentice relationship.

Obviously, the assistant's chances of learning a lot depend upon whether or not he or she is fortunate enough to land a job in a good studio that can provide the best possible experience.

Free-lance Assistants

But the assistant's choices are not limited to studio jobs. Many assistants work as free-lancers for a variety of photographers. Here, the first hurdle is to line up enough photographers to earn a respectable living. Many free-lancers earn about $50 a day in large cities, less in smaller localities, with some top assistants earning up to $70 or so per day.

The best thing about free-lancing is that it gives you a wide variety of experience. Since most free-lance assistants work less than five days a week, many averaging about three days, this leaves you plenty of time to work up a group of personal clients and shoot for them—being careful not to compete directly with photographers for whom you are working.

Some Tips from Former Assistants

Here are some tips from photographers' assistants who came up that route:

• If you are now a photography student, learn all you can while still in school about hardware, lighting, exposure, processing, and other basics. Also, try to develop some familiarity with real-life studio activities by hanging around a good local photographer's studio in your spare time.

• When going for an interview for a regular assistant's job, bring your portfolio and a resumé including previous experience and skills.

• Do not accept a job with a photographer who is not well organized and thoroughly professional. Bad habits are hard to break.

• Among the most important qualities photographers look for in an assistant are: eagerness to work hard and ability to learn fast; organization, poise, willingness to take orders, and a sense of how to anticipate the photographer's needs for equipment or materials.

• Do not be afraid to ask questions—but choose the right moment.

• Learn from mistakes made by other assistants in the studio and from the photographer. When you make one, inform the boss as soon as you discover it. Mistakes caught quickly can save a lot of time and money.

• Be willing to work overtime and on weekends.

• During the shooting session, keep checking the flash units, apertures and shutter-speed settings, and the background. If something is wrong, tell the photographer right away.

• Free-lance assistants should follow up on jobs by going back to the photographer for a look at the results of every shot they work on. This is an important final step in the assistant's education.

• Before you leave the ranks of assistants and take on all the duties of a professional photographer, be sure you are ready! Many a photographer has gone broke trying to equip a studio and get a business going before being able to count on enough income to pay the bills.

Where to Apply

If you feel that this is the approach to your career in photography, where do you go to look for a job?

The *Creative Black Book,* a comprehensive

country-wide listing of professionals, is considered the best list available. It includes nearly six hundred professionals under the "New York" heading, and hundreds more in other cities. It is published by Friendly Publications, 80 Irving Place, New York, N.Y. 10016. The last edition was priced at $11.

What Do Photographers Earn?

If you are becoming interested in photography as a career, you will want to know how much money photographers make. The following information will give you a rough idea.

Beginning photographers who work for newspapers that have a union contract with the Newspaper Guild earn between $150 and $450 a week. The more experienced press photographers get paid around $550 a week.

Photographers in the federal government earn about $16,000 a year. Trainees with the government begin at about $9,000; experienced government photographers go up to about $20,000.

Some self-employed and free-lance photographers are the highest paid in the field, and a few have become nationally known celebrities. However, the earnings of self-employed photographers can fluctuate greatly, as they are affected by general business conditions and by the type and size of the community and their ability to attract and hold customers.

Photographers in salaried jobs usually work a five-day, 35–40 hour week, with paid holidays, vacations, sick leave, and other benefits.

Those in business for themselves usually work

longer hours, but have more freedom in arranging their schedules.

Some Minus Features

Free-lance, press, and commercial photographers often travel frequently and may have to work in uncomfortable surroundings. Their work may often be hampered by unfavorable weather. Sometimes the work can be dangerous, especially for news photographers assigned to cover stories

It's a cold job, shooting aerial shots from the open door of a moving plane. The camera is semi-automatic, a special aerial type, which makes the job a bit easier. Aerial photographers generally use helicopters, or fairly slow-flying propeller planes.

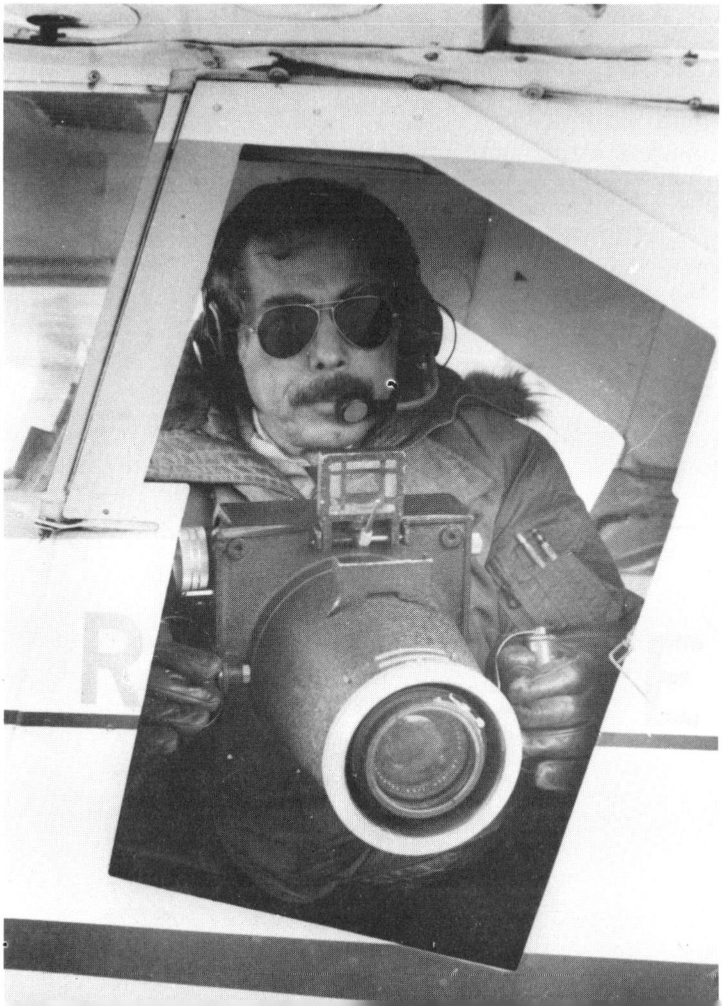

(Photo courtesy of Skyviews, Westbury, N.Y.)

on natural disasters or military conflicts, or for those doing underwater or aerial photography.

Animal Photography

Photographing animals is among the most demanding types of photography. There aren't very many men and women who seem to have the patience and the artistic skill to catch an animal in just the right pose. For those who do, this is a most rewarding career.

In addition to photographic skills, the animal photographer must have a strong sense of "human interest" values. He must be able to catch the character of the animal or animals he is shooting. He may often be called upon to get a photo of a person and a pet in a way that will tell a story in one picture.

Build a Portfolio

If you have an interest in animals, begin by taking shots of as many as you can, in black and white and in color. Practically all animal photography is on a free-lance basis, and most assignments are handed out by an editor or art director on the basis of a portfolio submitted by the photographer.

Before you begin trying experiments in animal photography, study the animal photographs in magazines, especially those of the pet food manufacturers.

One good tip is this: always have an assistant with you to catch the attention of the animal or animals you are shooting, and help you get natural poses.

If there are local dog or cat shows, you may get a chance to practice your animal photography, but always ask permission from one of the show officials. Most of the larger shows have "official" photographers with exclusive rights to take photos during the show.

When you have built up a portfolio that seems to meet professional standards, you can submit it to potential photo-purchasers in person or by mail, seeking assignments. You will be able to find the addresses of possible buyers in the market guides listings described in the Bibliography on page 126.

A Wide Field

While there are not too many good animal photographers in practice, there is wide demand for good animal photos.

For example, Walter Chandoha, one of the country's leading pet photographers, has had his work reproduced in countless magazine articles, has illustrated dozens of books, calendars, and novelty items, and has a huge collection of "stock" photos that get high prices from buyers or those wishing to reproduce them.

In the classified advertising sections of many magazines and newspapers, you will see ads of photographers who offer to come to your home and photograph your pet.

Don't think of animal photography as limited to pets. A number of photographers cover horse shows and the racing world. Some animal photographers with a scientific background devote themselves to wildlife photography, and you will find their work in such publications as *National Geographic, Scientific American, Nature,* and *The Smithsonian.*

Fashion Photography

In fashion photography, unlike portrait photography, the stress is on the clothes or accessories worn by the models.

Those who hire fashion photographers find it hard to describe just what they are looking for when they consider an applicant for a job. They want someone who combines the abilities of a photojournalist and an artist. The fashion photographer must be able to catch the model at the instant when the result will be a perfect photo, and the photo must be planned to hold a viewer's interest on the merchandise that is being displayed, not on the model.

Fashion photography is probably the most glamorous of all the fields of photography, and some top fashion photographers become internationally famous.

A number of schools offer courses in fashion photography, but competition in this field is incredibly tough. Perhaps the best way to break in is as assistant to an established photographer, but to get one of these coveted jobs takes both luck and connections.

A photography course with stress on fashion could help you get a job as an assistant in a fashion studio. In addition to a good fashion sense, you would be expected to have some familiarity with cameras and films used in the studio and on location, to be able to help in setting up lights and reflectors, to use a Polaroid or other instant camera for test shots, to be invisible when you are not

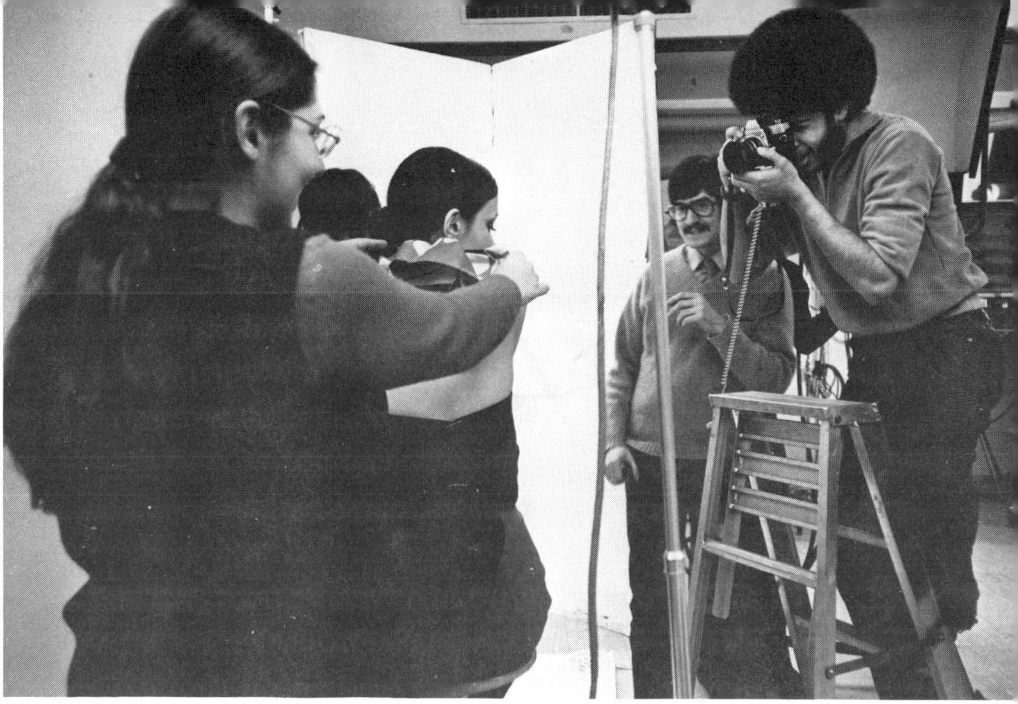

(Fashion Institute of Technology photo by John Senzer)

These students at New York's Fashion Institute of Technology are learning the techniques of fashion photography.

needed, and to be on hand immediately when you are.

A Bonus

One bonus of modern fashion photography is the opportunity to travel. Large stores and manufacturers rival each other in finding new locations to photograph their new styles.

For example, a recent advertisement for Neiman-Marcus of Dallas, Texas, said: "Where to go? At Neiman-Marcus, we search the world over for exciting backgrounds in which to present our fur collections. Last year found us high in the Andes, in Portillo, Chile. So this year, sea voyage seemed quite natural. Our choice, a Royal Viking cruise. Our party of fashion models, *photographers,* art directors, etc., boarded the ship. Ports of call:

Germany, Finland, Denmark, Sweden, and a sensational first, Russia." Most of the large New York City department stores shot their catalog photographs in equally exotic places.

Not all fashion photographers lead exciting jet-travel lives. Hundreds work, mostly in studios, for large organizations such as Sears, J.C. Penney, Montgomery-Ward, and other catalog houses. Hundreds of others work for the numerous mail-order houses which flood the mails with their catalogs just before Christmas each year, and for the photo studios that service such clients.

How to Break into the Field

You will have to show talent in the requirements of fashion photography, even for a beginner's job. What employers are seeking is photographers with a flawless eye for color, the patience and ability to meet the specific and precise requirements of advertisers, and the ingenuity to come up with exciting surprises in their photos.

As with other types of photography, you must begin your job hunt with a portfolio to show to an art director, an editor, or an agent who may be willing to represent you.

The prime requirement is an attractive model in poses ranging from high style to casual action. Show only your best work in the portfolio and limit it to a few dozen photos.

Also prepare some close-up photos of jewelry and accessories, to illustrate your ability in that area.

News Photography

On the opposite page, you can see a group of news photographers gathered to take shots of the ascent of a rocket carrying astronauts to the moon. But news photographers may also be assigned to cover a heated debate at a school board meeting, or the aftermath of an automobile accident or a fire.

Until a few years ago, news photography was an activity of the still photographer, but the development of the portable mini-cam has made it possible to cover spot news with motion-picture equipment, for TV broadcast. Changes in technology have opened wide career possibilities for news cameramen and women in photojournalism.

What Does It Take?

What are the personal attributes required to be a successful news photographer?

The National Press Photographers Association says that first is a deep sense of curiosity and an

This photograph shows some of the equipment used by news photographers for the launching of Apollo 8. More than 1300 photographers and news reporters covered this event.

(*NASA photo*)

(NASA photo)

News photographers line up to get shots of the landing of the Space Shuttle Orbiter *Enterprise* at the Flight Research Center in California. This picture was snapped while the *Enterprise* was still moving at very high speed.

interest in people—a desire to know more about their surroundings and their functions and the problems of their existence. It takes persistence to seek out more than one side of a situation, and requires an ability to put it into perspective with ongoing events.

Second is a measure of artistic aptitude to enable the photo reporter to organize images that will relate the facts of the story with emotional and visual qualities to attract the attention and interest of the viewers.

Third is sufficient mechanical aptitude to learn the photographic techniques required to get the images recorded on film with clarity and quality. For the experienced news photographer this requires a working knowledge of a wide variety of cameras, equipment, lenses and lighting gear, and

You can be pretty sure that this car was not stopped for a traffic violation. Police Department photographers are taking photos that may be used by detectives to investigate the crime, and may later be shown in court as evidence.

(*New York City Police Department photo*)

(*New York City Police Department photo*)

In a modern police department, one of the first specialists to arrive at a crime scene is the investigative photographer. With a little imagination, you can visualize what happened here.

an ability to choose the right equipment for the job at hand. Also needed is a thorough knowledge of laboratory processes used in producing reproductions from the latent images he brings back on film.

Is News Photography for You?

In addition, news photography requires flexibility and the ability to deal quickly with the unexpected—the sudden changes in routine created by unpredictable news events. Since news is a perishable commodity and must be fresh, the photographer must be able to work under pressure and expedite his newsphotos by the fastest means possible to meet the constant deadlines of publications and TV stations, and the efforts of his competitors.

The work requires a high degree of physical stamina. Breaking news stories may involve long hours of continuous work, or occur in locations which impose physical hardship to reach the scene of the action. While the equipment of the still photographer is generally quite portable, the television cameraman may have to shoulder a sound camera which can weigh 50 pounds or more.

There will be times when the assignment may not appeal to the photographer, or circumstances beyond his control may make it all but impossible to get the pictures that are wanted. The professional news photographer, however, will be required to produce top newsphotos in all kinds of weather conditions and at all times of day and night.

Education and Preparation

Some employers pay little attention to the educational background of photographers they hire—

the important consideration is the kind of photographs they turn in. Other employers look for job applicants with a college-level liberal arts background to give them better understanding of the stories to which they will be assigned.

As we noted in other chapters of this book, high school courses in basic photography are quite common. Many vocational photography courses are offered by community colleges, and now more and more universities are offering advanced training in photography. In their catalogs of courses, you will find departments of communications or fine arts which offer varied courses leading to degrees in television or photojournalism.

Some news photographers say they got their training in vocational schools, and a few through various home-study photography courses.

News photographers often developed their early interest as photographers for their high school newspapers or yearbooks. Contests like the ones described in this book will give you a measure of comparison for your work and a chance for recognition that will count when you apply for your first job.

Where Are the Jobs?

Jobs for photographers in this field exist on newspapers ranging from local weeklies to papers of national circulation; in television, from local stations to network news departments; with national news services and syndicates; and, in the magazine field, with many different kinds of publications.

However, for any job openings there is stiff competition. And many publications have few, if any,

(New York City Fire Department photo)

Fire Department photographers rush to the scene of suspicious blazes. Evidence like this, pictured on the spot, may lead to the conviction of an arsonist.

Waterfront fires are about the most difficult kind that New York City firemen face. Here, the Department photographer records the effects of the fire on 16mm motion-picture film.

(New York City Fire Department photo)

staff photographers but instead assign their work to free-lancers or photo agencies. For example, *Life* magazine, which reappeared in 1978 after going out of business in 1972, announced that it would not have staff photographers, but would assign all photo projects to free-lancers.

The college-educated person with photographic talent and interests may find jobs in what is now called the "communications" field. They can work as picture editors on newspapers or magazines, where they supervise the use of photos in the publication. In television, there are opportunities for film editors and production people with photographic or journalistic backgrounds.

For More Information

Two of the leading press photographers' organizations are:

The National Press Photographers Association
P.O. Box 1146
Durham, North Carolina 27701

Kappa Alpha Mu
201 Spring Valley Road
Columbia, Missouri 65201

Also, many large cities have local news photographers' groups. In some cities, these groups control the issuance of press identification cards to news photographers.

Theatrical Photographers

Are you stage-struck? If so, have you considered the possiblity of making your way into the world of the theater via the camera, rather than the stage?

What They Do

In front of any theater you will see large blow-ups showing members of the cast or scenes from the production. Those are just a small part of the theatrical photographer's efforts.

Publicity photos are sent out to newspapers and magazines. Some may be candid shots; others, posed studio portraits.

Actors and actresses—and those hoping to break into the theater—need portfolios of photos as part of their job-hunting strategy. The portfolio may include shots in different kinds of costumes and makeup, and all publicity shots call for a photographer who can really flatter his subject.

The photographer's part in a theatrical production begins as soon as the production goes into rehearsal. Often, shots taken during rehearsals are sent out in attempts to get publicity for the show. Many times, the photographs are taken after an evening performance. Some theatrical photographers estimate that they may take as many as 600 exposures during a musical performance, slightly fewer for a dramatic show.

Almost every job that a theatrical photographer does is a rush job. A "shooting session" may end about three in the morning, and the finished glossy prints of the pictures that are approved must be distributed early the next day.

How to Get into the Field

Here the problem is that theatrical photography is considered one of the glamour jobs and competition is keen. Those in the business say, "Get your training first, preferably in school, then try for an assistant's job with an established theatrical photographer."

In the yellow pages of the telephone directory you will find listings of many photographers who advertise that they do theatrical photography; you could try them.

Also, if there is an amateur or semiprofessional theatrical group in your community, they may welcome your offer to do their photography without charge and give you a chance to build up a portfolio, and perhaps some credit lines in the local papers if your pictures are used.

Above all, don't think that you will suddenly gain fame by shooting a Broadway show in New York. A typical big-city theatrical photographer can look back on years of preparation. One says he began by contributing photos to high school and college publications, then had four years' experience on a publication, followed by ten years as a picture editor, and finally recognition in the field of theatrical photography. You may also have to qualify for membership in a theatrical union before you can set foot on a professional stage with your camera.

For More Information

You can get more general information on careers in photography by writing to:

Eastman Kodak Company
Rochester, N.Y. 14650

Ask for the catalog of Special Career Materials.

Photographic Art & Science Foundation
111 Stratford Road
Des Plaines, Illinois 60016

Professional Photographers of America, Inc.
1090 Executive Way
Des Plaines, Illinois 60018

Also see the different organizations and publications mentioned in later chapters in this book, and publications listed in the Bibliography starting on Page 123.

(New York City Fire Department photo)

This photographer is recording the action of his colleagues fighting a blaze under the worst weather conditions.

3 / Related Occupations

In the Printing Industry

So far, most of the jobs that you read about in this book involve moving around with a camera and taking pictures. However, there are many other types of occupations related to photography.

For example, it has been estimated that there are about 10,000 jobs in the printing industry that require a knowledge of photography. Many of these jobs might be of interest to persons with handicaps that limit their ability to move around rapidly.

In recent years, more and more commercial printers and publications have changed over to use of photographic type and offset reproduction, which are basically photographic processes.

In the modern printing industry, among the highest-paid craftsmen are photoengraving cameramen, offset cameramen, strippers, printers, etchers, and finishers.

Most persons in these crafts learn the skill through a five-year apprentice program, which includes at least 800 hours of classroom instruction. Apprenticeship applicants must be at least eighteen years of age and usually must have a high school education or its equivalent, preferably with courses in chemistry and physics. Many employers require a physical examination for apprentices. Good eyesight is particularly important because of the close work and color discrimination needed.

For More Information

For facts about employment and apprentice programs in this field, write to:

Graphic Arts Technical Foundation
4615 Forbes Avenue
Pittsburgh, Pennsylvania 15213

You will also find information on this kind of work in this author's book *You Can Be a Printer* (Lothrop, Lee & Shepard Company, 105 Madison Avenue, New York, N. Y. 10016.)

Laboratory Technician

Most professional photographers make limited use of the self-developing cameras. Often they use one to make a test shot to find out how a layout looks, before they proceed to shoot it with their regular equipment. The negatives are sent to a laboratory for development and printing. In addition to the professional work, it has been estimated that about 6½ billion pictures a year are taken by amateurs, making photo printing a huge industry.

In addition to thinking of photo-lab work as a full-time job, you can also think of it as an asset to a working photographer. Many small publications and in-plant operations would have openings for photographers who could do their own darkroom work.

While most amateur photographs are processed by automatic equipment, providing jobs for less skilled technicians, there has also been a move in the other direction. In many cities there are "custom" laboratories which work exclusively for professional photographers, providing the services of expert technicians, printers and processors, for

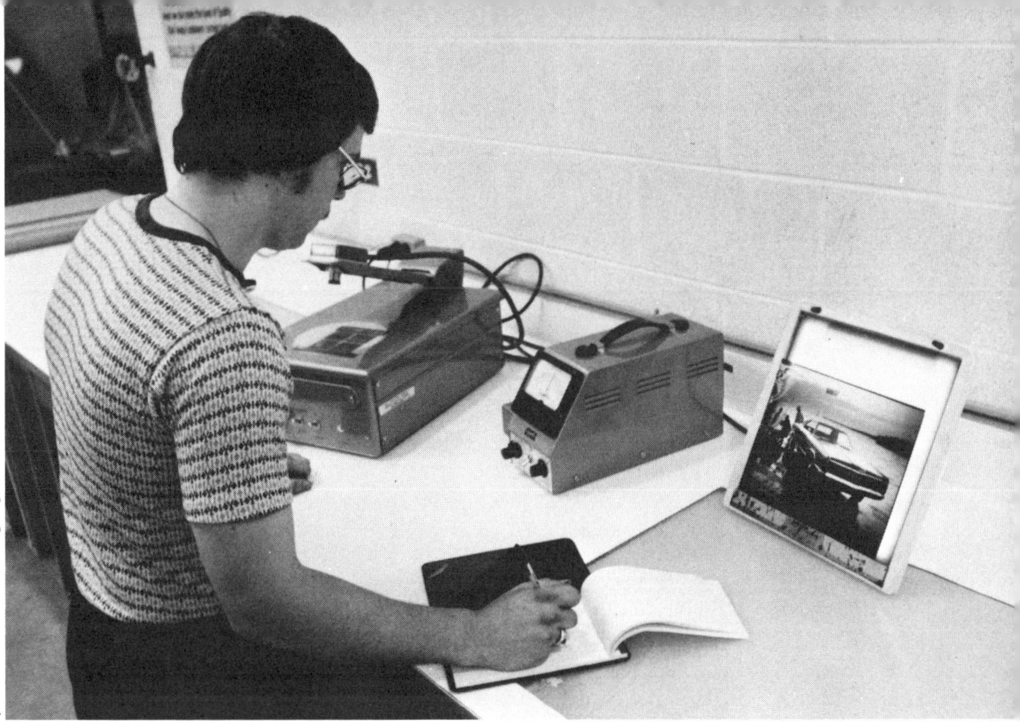
(Ferris State College photo)

Against a light frame, this student can judge the quality of his transparency.

high-quality black-and-white or color photographs and enlargements.

What the Work Is Like

Developing black-and-white negative film requires five steps: developer, stop bath, fixing bath, washing, and drying. The first three steps use chemical solutions and are performed in darkness. After unwinding a roll of film, the technician places it in the developer, a solution that brings out the image on exposed film. After the film has remained in the developer for a specified period, the technician transfers it to a stop bath to prevent overdevelopment. Next, the film is placed in a fixing bath that makes it insensitive to light, thus preventing further exposure. Finally, the technician washes the film with water to remove the fixing

(Ferris State College photo)

This projector blows up prints many times their size, so the student photographer can examine every part of the picture she took.

solution and places the film in a drying cabinet or on a drying drum.

Processes for developing color film are more complex. The technician makes a photograph by transferring the image from a negative to photographic paper. Printing is frequently performed on a projection printer, which consists of a fixture for holding negatives and photographic paper, an electric lamp, and a magnifying lens. The technician places the negative between the lamp and lens, and the paper below the lens. When he turns on the lamp, light passes through the negative and lens and records a magnified image of the negative on the paper. During printing, the technician may vary the contrast of the image or remove unwanted background by using his hands or paper patterns to shade part of the photographic paper from the projected image. After removing the exposed photographic paper from the printer, he develops it in much the same way as the negative. If the customer desires, the technician mounts the finished print in a frame or on a paper or cardboard back.

How to Become a Lab Technician

Most darkroom technicians learn their skills through informal on-the-job training. Beginners start as helpers, and gradually learn to develop and print film by assisting experienced technicians. It generally takes three to four years to become a fully qualified technician.

It is also possible to prepare for the work in

The lights were on to take this shot, but this is a typical school darkroom setup. These students are in a class at California College of Arts and Crafts in Oakland, California.

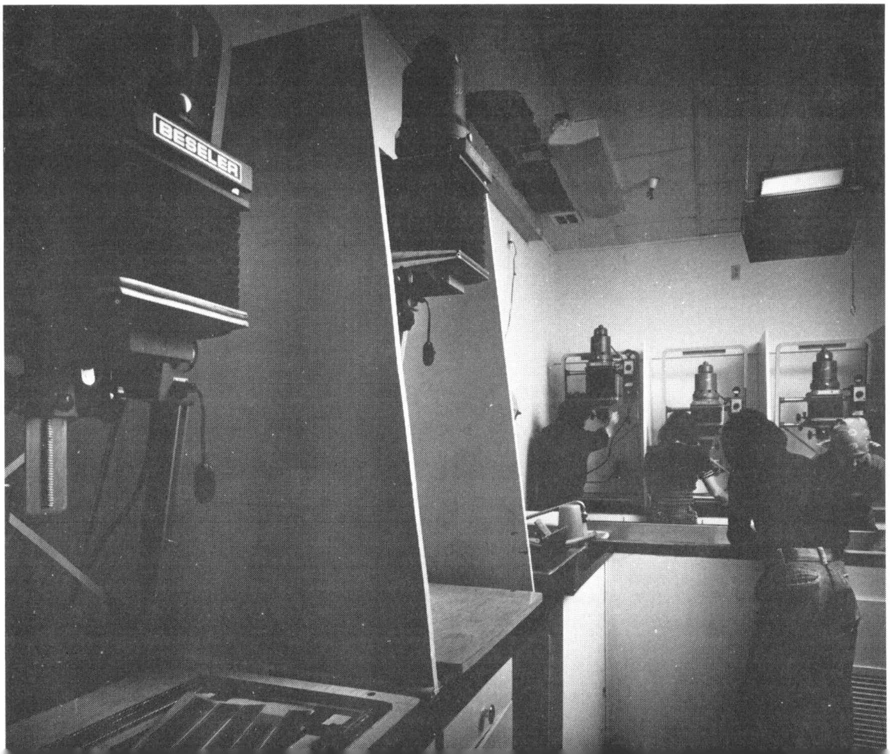

(California College of Arts and Crafts photo)

school. Some high schools and trade schools offer courses in photography that include training in film processing, and it can also be learned in the armed forces.

Two-year courses leading to a degree in photographic technology are offered by a few colleges, and completion of these courses may be helpful in leading to jobs such as supervisor or manager of a photo lab.

One interesting note is that some laboratories use blind persons as film numberers and film strippers, since these jobs are performed in the dark to prevent light damage to exposed film.

For More Information

Information about employment opportunities in photographic laboratories and about schools that offer degrees in photographic technology is available from:

Master Photo Dealers' and Finishers' Association
603 Lansing Avenue
Jackson, Michigan 49202

Professional Photographers of America, Inc.
1090 Executive Way
Des Plaines, Illinois 60018

Camera Repairer

As cameras become more complicated, there are more things that can go wrong with them, and more and more cameras end up in the hands of a camera repairer.

Many camera repairers learn the job by working in a camera retail shop or in a photographic manufacturing plant where cameras and other photographic equipment are made. However, so many of the cameras now in use are imported that the opportunity to get a job in the manufacturing part of the business is very limited.

The photographer who can repair his own equipment is in an enviable position. However, many repair jobs call for special tools and techniques. A beginning camera repairer with some background and training can start at about $150 a week, and with experience can earn well over $400 a week. The U.S. Army and Navy train their photographers in repair work.

Camera Repair and Mechanics Course

A course in camera repair is one of the most demanding in the photographic field. The repair person must understand camera operation and construction, mechanical and electronic. He or she must be familiar with accessory equipment and

(California College of Arts and Crafts photo)

The head of the media center looks on while the film librarian does her job. Note the handy clippers to cut portions of her film that may not be up to par.

operations, and must have a basic knowledge of photography and the needs of the photographer. He or she must be familiar with all types of hand and power tools, and should be able to make special tools and parts, especially for complicated imported cameras.

A complete course in this field would take about 350 class hours.

For More Information

For information on schools which teach camera repair, write to:

National Association of Trade and Technical Schools
2021 L Street N.W.
Washington, D.C. 20036

Note that before signing up for a course with any school, you are entitled to know the following: length of the course; full tuition and refund policy, should you have to drop out; information as to the school's facilities; what percentage of the school's graduates are actually employed in the job for which the school trains them.

4/A Business of Your Own?

Some Hazards

If you think you are a pretty good photographer, and your friends agree with you, then you may have the idea of starting your own photographic business. When you reach the age of eighteen you are legally an adult, and can sign contracts and leases, apply for credit, and run a business.

When it comes to business, a contract signed by an eighteen-year-old is fully valid in most states. In Hawaii, there is no age restriction; in three states, Alabama, Nebraska, and Wyoming, the age is nineteen. (However, married Nebraskans under age nineteen have full majority status.)

However, there are some dangers in getting started in your own photographic business. One pitfall is to take the compliments of friends and relatives too seriously. It is one thing to be a very good photographer according to the standards of the novice or the advanced amateur. But when you start earning your living by photography, you become a professional and your work will be judged by professional standards. You will be competing with people who may be well known, who have had years of experience, and who do superior photographic work consistently, not just occasionally.

Starting your own photographic business is an idea which should be examined critically before you embark on this course of action.

(3M Company photo)

Professionals like these know just what they want before they will use a photo. Are you sure you are good enough to satisfy them?

Even being a very good photographer does not ensure success as a photographer, much less as an owner of a studio or other photographic business. One common error is this: As an amateur photographer, you may add up the cost of photographic equipment and materials and decide you can make a good profit at prices much lower then those charged by the professional photographer in your neighborhood.

In practice, however, photographic equipment and materials are often among the smaller items on a photographer's budget. You should consider other costs of running a business: salaries, outside services you will need, rent, heat, electricity, taxes, insurance, advertising, and the frequent problem of customers who do not pay their bills.

The Kodak Company, which has had long experience in the field of photography, says that it is not unusual for beginning photographers to go into business for themselves, but it is unusual for them to stay in business. They suggest that it is better to try your talents as a free-lance photographer, or try to get a job in the kind of photographic business you'd like to own, and learn as much as possible that way.

On the other hand, some young people have started their own photographic businesses and have been successful.

A Checklist

Looking ahead to the time when you will be ready to plunge into the business world, ask yourself these questions:

1. Will you have had any actual business experience?
2. Have you figured how much time you will need until the business income equals the expenses?
3. Can you estimate how much you could earn from your business?
4. How does this compare with what you could earn at a job?
5. Have you counted up how much money you will have to invest in your business?
6. Would you have some cash on hand for unexpected needs?
7. Would you be willing to risk uncertain or irregular income for several years?

8. Would you be qualified to supervise the buying and selling for your business?

9. Will you be able to determine what prices you will have to charge to compare favorably with prices charged by competitors?

10. Have you discussed your plans with any persons who know enough about the kind of business to give you worthwhile advice?

If you really feel that a business of your own in photography is your goal, then good luck! Meanwhile, the U.S. Government has dozens of pamphlets and books about going into and running a small business; many are free on request.

For More Information

For information on these, ask for a list of Small Business Administration publications from:

Office of Information
Small Business Administration
1441 L Street N.W.
Washington, D.C. 20416

How About a Camera Shop?

A United States Government publication says, "The face of the United States is freckled with small camera shops. This has come about largely because new, easy-to-use equipment and materials have created widespread interest in photography as a hobby."

Often, especially in smaller towns, the operator of the local camera shop is also a working photographer. For example, in the small town where this author lives, the camera shop owner is an active photographer. Part of the store is set up as a small studio, where he takes passport and other I.D. photographs, and wedding photos and other types of portrait work. He is also the photographer for the local weekly newspaper, and is called upon for any needed publicity, industrial, or commercial photographs. The two parts of his business seem to help each other. His frequent byline under photographs reminds readers of his shop, and the presence of the shop leads people to call on him when they need a photographer or when they have films to develop and print.

Are You a Good Teacher?

Are you a good teacher? This may seem a strange question to ask yourself when you are considering a future as a camera shop owner-photographer. But even the modern, easy-to-use photographic equipment may seem frightening to a novice. They see the array of cameras and accessories and may feel that it would take someone with an engineering education to take pictures.

Many new photo hobbyists feel that only in a

The use of lights makes all the difference in portrait photography. Here a student has adjusted the lights and hopes that the picture will do justice to his subject.

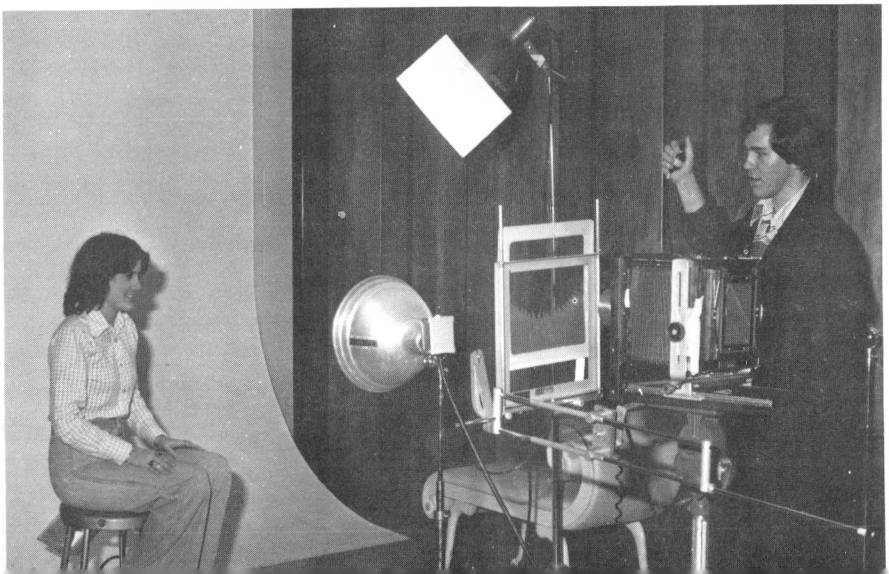

(VICA photo)

camera store will they get reliable instructions. As the store operator, you must have unlimited patience. A novice may be slow to grasp a point that seems elementary to you. You must be able to explain the operation of any piece of equipment you sell, in simple, non-technical language.

How do you think you would rate as a teacher?

The Trusty Screwdriver

Minor camera repairs are a part of the life of the shop owner. Will you know enough about cameras to handle simple repair jobs?

Many customers will rush in with what seems to be a major problem. It often turns out to be a trifle to one who knows photographic equipment and is handy with a screwdriver. A two-minute repair job may make a customer for life. Because the camera business is highly technical, only people who understand it and have the skills needed to handle the sometimes complex equipment are likely to enter it. But technical skill alone does not qualify a camera buff as a merchant. You must also have the ability and knowledge to manage a business.

What Are Your Chances of Success?

Not all retail camera shops are successful or making large profits, but those who survive the first couple of years usually prosper. The most frequent causes of failure are: (1) inexperienced management, (2) trying to meet discount competition head on, (3) radical changes in the local employment situation, (4) poor location, and (5) a higher salary for the owner than the business can afford.

But interest in taking snapshots is growing. People are buying more—and more expensive—cameras and supplies. Your chances for success in a small retail shop are good, if you (1) know your business both as a cameraman and as a business manager, (2) can combine it with profitable photographic work, (3) have a good location, (4) are willing to put in the effort and have the money needed for a start, and (5) limit your income to what you can draw from the profits of the business.

Keeping Informed

If you think that your future goal might lie in becoming a photographer-shop owner, you can begin by preparing yourself for that career. In other parts of this book we have covered different ways of learning photography. Owning-managing a retail camera shop calls for a wide range of knowledge in order to have a good chance of success.

You will have to be informed about new products, new techniques, new merchandising methods, and the basics of running a business. In many cities, public and private schools offer courses in business administration, as do some correspondence schools, and it could be worthwhile to enroll in one of these courses.

You may get some good ideas just from walking through camera stores with a keen eye. The trade magazines for camera-store operators are usually full of ideas for the retailer. Two of these are:

Photo Marketing, 603 Lansing Avenue, Jackson, Michigan 49202, a monthly magazine that is the official publication of the Master Photo Dealers' and Finishers' Association.

Photo Weekly, 1 Astor Plaza, New York, N.Y. 10036, deals with the business aspect of photographic shops.

A government publication that may give you good leads to study material in this field is *Small Business Bibliography No. 64: Photographic Dealers and Studios,* free from the Small Business Administration, 1441 L Street N.W., Washington, D.C. 20416, or from one of SBA branch offices located in cities all over the country. You will find them in your telephone directory, under "United States Government" listings.

5/How You Can Prepare Now for a Career in Photography

If you are in junior or senior high school, the information on the following pages has been written with you in mind.

Scouting Programs

There are different ways in which you can begin getting some background in photography and, perhaps most important, begin finding out whether you really have the ability and the desire to go ahead in that kind of work.

Both the Boy Scouts and the Girl Scouts have merit badge programs in photography. It happens that reading this book may help you meet one of the requirements for the merit badge!

The Boy Scout merit badge pamphlet *Photography* lists the requirements to qualify for the badge as follows:

1. Tell what makes a good picture. Show your understanding of these principles as you take pictures for requirement 2.
2. Do EITHER *a* or *b*.
   a. Take 10 good black-and-white or color pictures. Do the following:
      1) Take from three to five of these ten pictures indoors with a flash.
      2) Take at least five of the ten pictures so they tell a story.

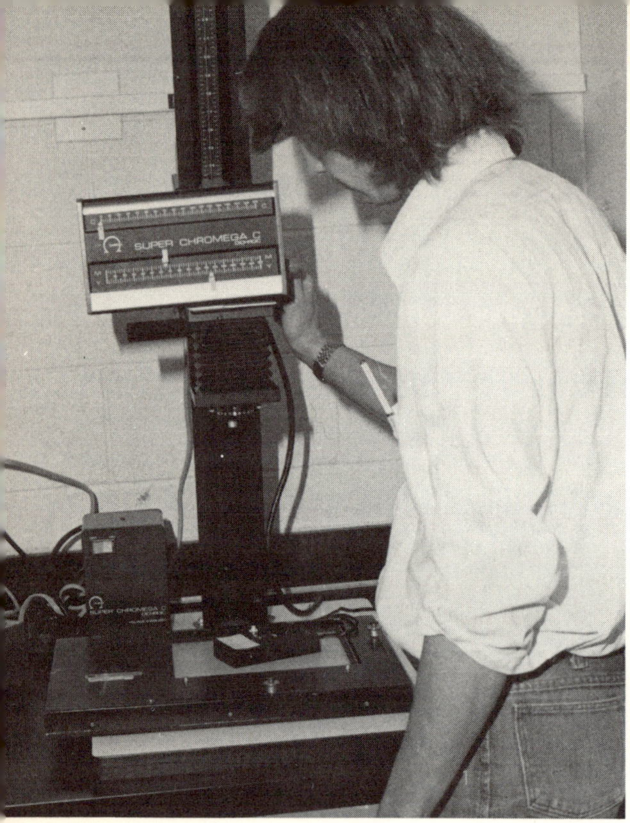

(VICA photo)

In professional camera work, you can't guess at things. This student is making careful checks before using an enlarger.

3) Show your pictures to your counselor in an organized way.

b. Make planning cards and take 50 feet of movie film. Do the following

1) Edit your film so that you have at least 25 feet of quality movies that tell a story.

2) Show your film to your counselor.

3. Make a pinhole camera. Explain how it works. Obtain one finished print taken with your pinhole camera. Compare it with a print of the same scene which you took with a regular camera. Explain the differences.

4. Explain how photographic film is processed. Tell how black-and-white prints are made.

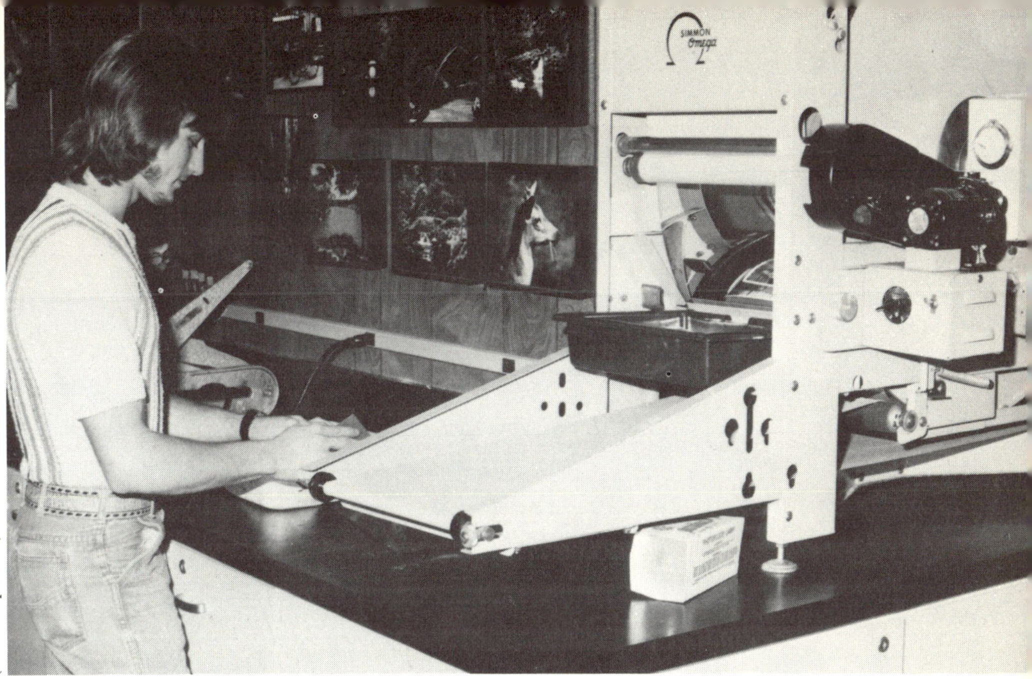

(VICA photo)

Drying black-and-white prints is more or less automatic, but the operator has to keep an eye on the drying drum to be sure it's working properly.

5. Explain common photographic terms such as lens, shutter, viewfinder, camera angle, exposure, negative, transparency, *f*-number, and planning card.
6. Describe jobs in photography.

More advanced scouting-photography programs are offered by the Explorers—the young adult division of the BSA, which includes both young men and young women in its membership.

The Explorers' director says that there are 122 Explorer posts in the United States with 1,398 members specializing in photography.

To find out about this activity in your neighborhood, phone your local Scouting center. You will find it listed in your telephone directory, under "Boy Scouts of America."

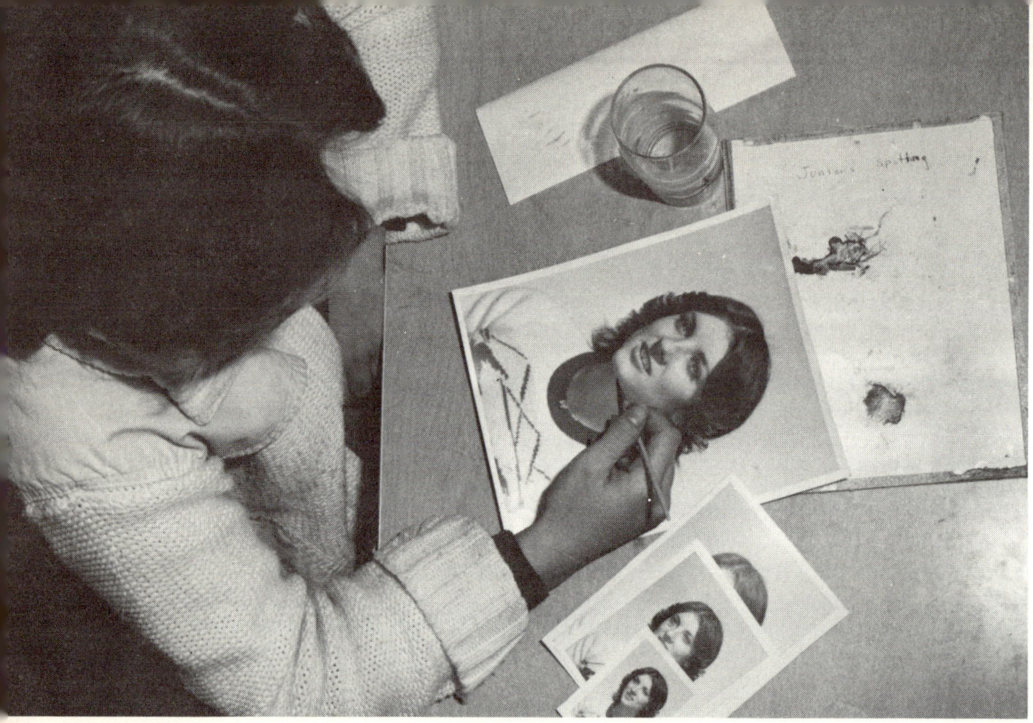
(VICA photo)

When a picture is finished, the photo retoucher can still add little touches to improve it.

What the Girl Scouts Do

The Girl Scouts of America have a somewhat similar program in photography, but they seem to put more stress on the artistic aspects of photography.

As their handbook says, "Taking a picture may be your way of writing a poem, telling a story, expressing a mood. The camera lens may be your eye, through which you see and record your special world. For photography can be more than a mechanical matter of shutter-snapping. In the world of an artist, it is an art.

"To appreciate this, you have only to look at pictures made by imaginative contemporary photographers. Look for the work of such artists in your library or a museum. Then you will see what really creative photography can be.

"How much do you have to know to take artistic pictures? Actually, a simple, inexpensive camera can make poetry for you if you turn it upon subjects that mean something to you. As you progress, you will be quicker to catch subjects, more sensitive to designs of light and shadow, traceries of trees, expressions of people.

"The more you know about photography, the more you can do, the greater your satisfaction. Books and magazines can help you learn.

"But your greatest satisfaction will come when you take pictures with a sense of artistry and deep feeling."

Requirements for the Merit Badge

The eight requirements for the Girl Scout merit badge in photography are:

1. Load your camera with film. After you have finished using the film, unload it. Explain the parts of your camera as you use it or adjust it to take a picture.
2. Make a list of the subjects you plan to photograph. Tell how far away you will stand from each.
3. Show a photograph that tells a story. Explain why it tells a story.
4. Explain how foreground or background objects can help or spoil a picture.
5. Take a time exposure or flash picture.
6. Take a series of pictures of the same subject showing variation in light and shadow: light be-

hind the object, light behind the camera, light from the side, through a doorway or branches, close up, far away.

7. Take pictures to use as a record of a trip or event OR take pictures to tell a story and choose a title for the story.

8. Mount one or two of your best pictures OR start a photograph album. Write captions for the pictures.

Girl Scout Photography Awards

Each year the Girl Scouts of America and the Eastman Kodak Company sponsor a photography awards program. Entrants are divided into three classes, Girl Scouts aged 6–12, those aged 13–17, and adults affiliated with the organization.

Both color and black-and-white photographs are eligible for awards. Each person may enter as many as three color and three black-and-white photographs. Color and black-and-white photographs will be judged separately. Only photographs taken after June 1 of the previous year will be eligible.

A $500 U.S. Savings Bond will be awarded for the most outstanding photograph, color or black-and-white in each age category.

Second award will be a $100 U.S. Savings Bond in each category for color and black-and-white photographs.

Two $50 U.S. Savings Bonds will be similarly awarded, and merit awards will be granted for other photographs selected by the panel of judges.

For information and entry forms, write to:

How to Enter

Girl Scout Photography Awards
Girl Scouts of the U.S.A.
830 Third Avenue
New York, N.Y. 10022

We mentioned earlier in this book that many high schools give courses in photography and even more have camera clubs.

But there is one organization in almost 9,000 high schools in the United States—perhaps in your school—that works with students who are considering photography as their future life-work.

The VICA Program

This is VICA, which stands for Vocational Industrial Clubs of America—sort of a fraternity and sorority for high school students who are taking vocational courses, or are planning careers in industrial work.

In many states the VICA clubs have a yearly competition for the best photographic work by club members.

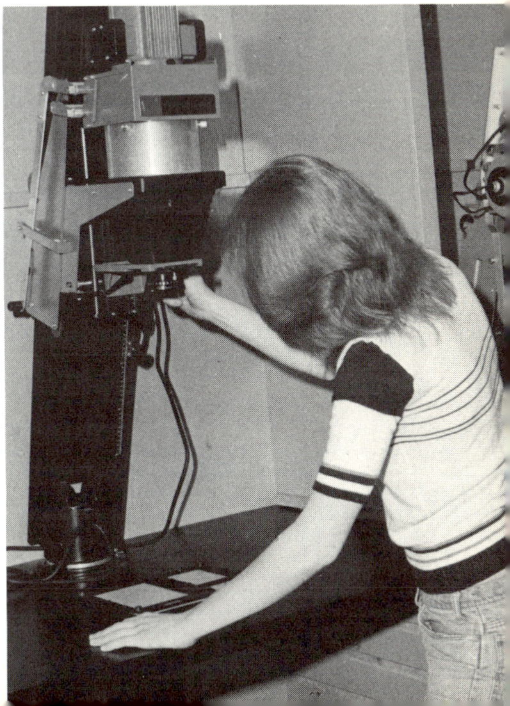

(VICA photo)

Enlarging photos is tricky. Here a VICA student is learning the technique.

VICA Trade Vocations

VICA clubs cover a wide range of vocations in addition to photography. They are:

Air-conditioning mechanic
Aircraft mechanic
Appliance repairman
Auto-body repairman
Auto mechanic
Bricklayer
Building maintenance man
Cabinetmaker
Carpenter
Cement mason
Commercial artist
Cook
Cosmetologist
Dental assistant
Diesel mechanic
Draftsman
Dressmaker
Dry cleaner
Electrician
Fireman
Fishery occupations
Food trade worker
Instrument repairman
Ironworker
Janitor
Jeweler and watchmaker
Laboratory assistant
Launderer
Machinist
Maintenance mechanic
Meatcutter
Medical assistant
Nurse's aide
Optical mechanic
Painter
Paperhanger
Patternmaker
Pipe fitter
Plasterer
Plumber
Practical nurse
Presser
Printer
Radio and television repairman
Sewing machine operator
Sheet-metal worker
Shipbuilding
Shoe repairman
Tailor
Textile worker
Tile setter
Tool and die maker
Welder

If you are interested in VICA, find out whether there is a chapter in your school that works on photography. If there is not, speak to your school counselor, or write for more information to:

Vocational Industrial Clubs of America
105 North Virginia Avenue
Falls Church, Virginia 22046

The VICA club in the Tulsa County (Oklahoma)

How the Club Works

Area Vocational-Technical School has a two-year program starting in grade eleven. The theory covers such subjects as light, optics, chemistry of photography, rules of composition, photographic printing, and the use of various cameras.

Practical projects are provided to familiarize students with modern techniques and methods used in photography. The photography students cover all of the activities of VICA, using both black-and-white and color film: the sweetheart contests, leadership and skill contests, election of class officers, special projects, and human interest stories.

The VICA motto is, "Preparing for Leadership in the World of Work." The student photographers use their skills to tell the story of VICA with photography.

The eleventh-grade student works strictly in black-and-white and learns to use all types of professional equipment, develop film, and make black-and-white prints—all this in addition to textbook study of terms, definitions, and equipment. The twelfth-grade student learns to work in color, using color negative materials and positive materials (slides) and using the more advanced equipment.

Advanced students take pictures, develop the film, and make color prints which are finished in a professional manner. During the last nine weeks of their senior year, VICA tries to find them part-time work in photography. The employer then grades them on their work.

One way to find out whether you really are a

(*Scholastic/Kodak Photography Awards photo*)

These are some of the winners in the Scholastic/Kodak Award Contest. Does your photography come near the quality they show? "Earthquake," by Scott Headley, 15, from Greece Arcadia High School, Rochester, N.Y., won the Kodak Medallion of Excellence in 1977.

This color shot was one of the winners of an Honor Award for color in the 1977 competition. It was by Dan Allyn, 14, Tillicum Junior High School, Bellevue, Washington.

(*Scholastic/Kodak Photography Awards photo*)

(Scholastic/Kodak Photography Awards photo)

This Honor Award photo from the 1973 competition was taken by Deni Obermire, 17, from Lompoc Senior High School, Lompoc, California.

(Scholastic/Kodak Photography Awards photo)

This experimental and creative design, "Hair in the Air," won an Honor Award in black-and-white for Charlie Clement, 18, from Rham High School in Hebron, Connecticut, in 1977.

Scholastic/Kodak Contest

good photographer is through the Scholastic Magazines/Eastman Kodak Company yearly Photography Awards Program. Winning one of the awards will certainly help when you apply for your first job. There are also scholarship grants, cash prizes, and honorable mention certificates.

Another Honor Award photo for Experimental and Creative Design in the 1977 competition was won by Kevin Knepp, 18, from James Whitcomb Riley High School, South Bend, Indiana.

(*Scholastic/Kodak Photography Awards photo*)

The contest is open to junior and senior high school students in the United States and Canada. Kodak awards one $1,000 scholarship grant to the high school senior who enters the best portfolio of twelve photographs, and a $500 grant to the second choice of the judges. Other prizes include cash awards totaling about $6,000, Awards of Excellence, Honor Awards, and Honorable Mention Certificates.

The award-winning photographs are displayed at the Kodak Gallery in New York City, and the awards are widely publicized. This means that the winners' names, and often their best photographs, appear in local newspapers.

The principal's office in your school most probably will have information on this contest, and entry blanks.

If your school does not have the information and forms, write to:

Scholastic Photography Awards
50 West 44th Street
New York, N.Y. 10036

PSA/RIT Scholarship

The Photographic Society of America (PSA) each year offers a $1,500 scholarship to the Rochester Institute of Technology (RIT), one of the country's leading colleges in photographic studies.

The general requirement is, "High school graduates with an aptitude for and interest in photography may apply" for the scholarship to the Rochester, New York, college.

Graduating seniors and those who have graduated from high school within the preceding two years are eligible.

First, they must have applied and been accepted as a freshman into one of the following courses at RIT:

Photographic Illustration
Photographic Science and Instrumentation
Professional Photography
Biomedical Photography/Biomedical Photographic Communications.

Rochester Institute of Technology was founded in 1829, and is a fully accredited college with a student enrollment of about 7,000. It awards a bachelor of science degree (B.S.) in photographic studies and a bachelor of fine arts degree (B.F.A.) in photographic illustration.

Requests for information concerning admission to RIT should be made to the Director of Admissions:

Mr. E. Louis Guard
Rochester Institute of Technology
One Lomb Memorial Drive
Rochester, New York 14623

Applications for the scholarship should be made before December 1 to:

Robert D. Routh, APSA
Chairman
PSA Education/Scholarship Committee
842 South Helena Street
Anaheim, California 92805

Other Scholarships and Aid Programs

Many colleges and universities throughout the

United States and Canada offer scholarships that are available for students who want to take photographic courses. In addition, there are many tuition-free community and state colleges.

Perhaps the best first step in planning your college studies in photography is to get a copy of a booklet that is published by Eastman Kodak Company and is revised every few years. Called *A Survey of Motion Picture, Still Photography, and Graphic Arts Instruction,* it lists all American and Canadian colleges, universities, technical institutes, and schools of photography, and lists the courses they offer.

For a copy of this booklet, write to:

Motion Picture and Audiovisual Markets Division
Eastman Kodak Company
Rochester, New York 14650

The present price of the book is sixty-five cents.

When you have that book, pick out that college or school that seems to meet your needs and write to the Director of Admissions there. Ask for their catalog of photographic courses, and information on scholarships and student-aid programs. You should do this very early in your senior year in high school, or before.

A recent study by Eastman Kodak showed that more than 1,600 students in the United States and Canada were receiving scholarships or other forms of student assistance in photographic courses.

6/What You Learn in Photography Courses

The courses you take in photography will cover pretty much the same ground whether you take them at a school of photography or at a college. However, the advantage of the college curriculum is that it will give you a more rounded education, with classes in academic subjects in addition to photography.

A Basic Course

The following details on the course in Commercial Photography offered by the Germain School in New York City will give you a good idea of what a photography course covers, and also what the photographer must know in order to operate as a professional. This 270-hour course is described as preparing those who complete it for self-employment, an entry-level position as a black-and-white photographer, or a technician in any area of commercial photography. The following topics are covered:

Fundamentals

Cameras, Lenses, Focusing, Apertures, Shutters, Exposure Principles, Films, Basic Camera Techniques, Negative Processing (sheet films), Contact Printing, Enlarging, Viewpoint, Elementary Lighting, Principles of Contrast Control, Lighting Contrast, Developmental Contrast, Use of Exposure Meters, Depth of Field, Perspective Control, View Camera Swings and Tilts, Projection Printing Controls, Printing Papers, Print Spotting, Negative Emulsions, Nature of Light, Filters, Copying Principles, Basic Optics, Photographic Chemistry, Reduction, Intensification, Negative Analysis, Flash Principles, Electronic Flash (studio type), Print Mounting, Visual Thinking, The Polaroid Process, Motion Control, Available Light.

Small Camera Techniques
Camera Types, Lenses, Accessory Features, Negative Processing (roll films), Fine Grain Processing, Available Light, Portable Electronic Flash, Motion Control, Tonal Values, Attitudes and Conceptualization.

Commercial Techniques
Layouts, Composition, Advanced Lighting Techniques, Textures, Painting with Light, Shadowless Lighting, Contouring, Separation, Photomacrography, Montage, Model Direction, Catalog Illustration, Full-length Fashion, Fashion Accessories, Architectural Exteriors and Interiors, Industrial, Landscapes, News, Feature, Legal, Social Commentary, Importance of Viewpoint, Outdoor Still Life.

Subjects photographed may include jewelry, tools, tableware, food, beverages, drugs, tobacco, cosmetics, stemware, cut glass, antiques, ceramics, clothing, flowers, buildings, animals, machinery,

(Washington Technical Institute photo)

The layout artist uses artistic skills to get the most out of a photograph on the page of a publication.

and people, pictured and captured at work and at play, active and in repose.

Portfolio Preparation and Critique

The student is responsible for preparing two portfolios—one of work done in the studio under the direction of the instructor; the other of personal work done on location with the student's own camera.

Other Courses

Other courses with emphasis on preparing for

specialized photographic work might include: Portrait Illustration and Lighting; Motion Picture Photography; Forensic (Criminalistics) Photography; Fashion Photography; Photojournalism; Advertising Illustration; Industrial Photography; Videotape Techniques; and specialized courses in Color Photography.

Cooperative Degree Programs

Some colleges have joined hands with vocational photography schools to provide vocational training in photography, plus a college degree.

Typical is the program offered by St. John's University and the Germain School of Photography, both in New York City.

The student takes his academic studies at St. John's, and technical training in photography at Germain. Germain's General Professional Career Photography course gives thirty credits toward an Associate in Science, Bachelor of Science, or Bachelor of Fine Arts degree. Usually the Germain photography courses are completed first and the student then attends classes at one of the St. John's University campuses.

Courses at both these schools are given in day and evening sessions. An accelerated day course allows students, after they have completed their photographic course requirements, to obtain an A.S. degree in 1½ years, and a B.S. or B.F.A. in 3½ years.

If a program like this interests you, write to the college or colleges that appeal to you, and ask whether they have such a program.

7/ Jobs in Government

It sometimes seems that government could not function without cameras. Almost every time an official or high-level politician does anything, it is done to the accompaniment of flash bulbs and strobe lights and TV mini-cams.

Practically every agency of government from the White House down to county or municipal offices will have some kind of photographic department.

How Photographers Are Hired

How do you get these jobs?

On the local level, photographers are usually hired on an informal basis. The person with photographic background and local connections may be hired. Many of the lower-level jobs may be on a part-time basis, and the photographer for a local newspaper or magazine may moonlight as a photographer for the local government or department.

Usually on the county or state level, photographers are hired on a more formal basis through civil service procedure. Applicants for job openings as photographers must file a written application listing experience and any training in photography they may have completed, and then may have to pass a written and sometimes a performance test in photography before they can be hired.

For information on photography jobs in state

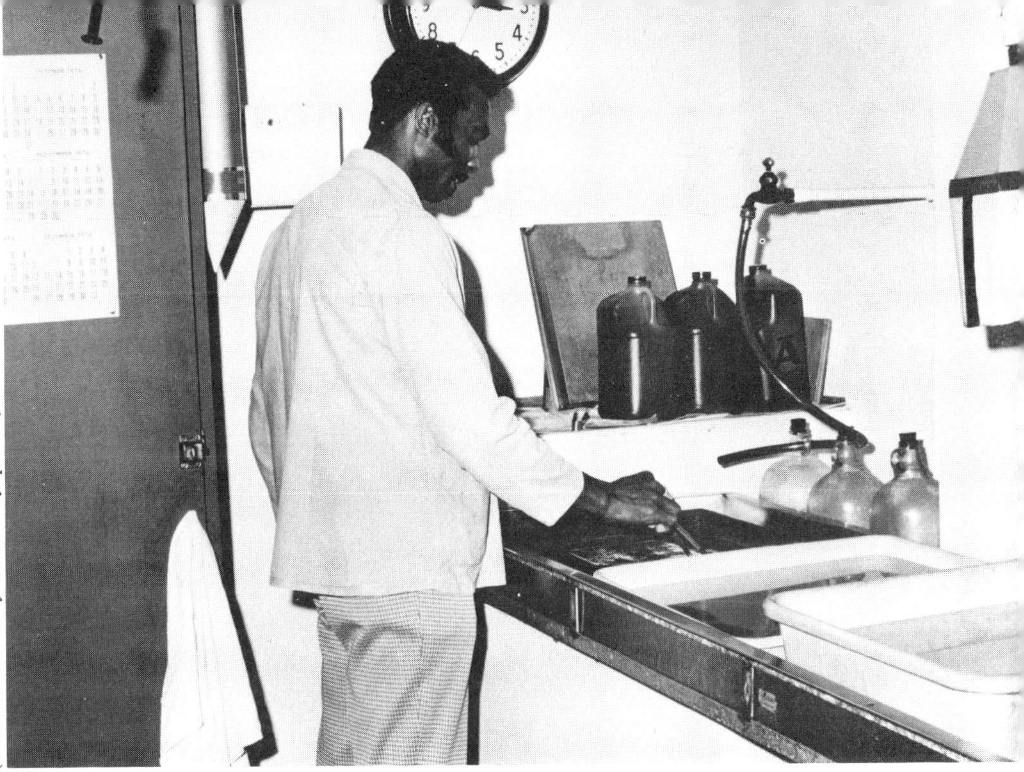

(Tennessee Valley Authority photo)

This technician is developing black-and-white prints.

and county civil service, write to the Civil Service Commission or Bureau of Personnel at your state capitol.

Opportunities in the Federal Government

While it is hard to get an exact figure, it is believed that the federal government is the largest employer of photographers in the United States.

Every large government agency and bureau has a public relations or information staff, which means a need for photographers to provide photos for newspapers, books, and magazines, and for publications by the department. For example, many of the photographs in this book were provided by government photographers.

The U.S. Government Printing Office is one of

(U.S. Department of Agriculture photo by Jack Schneider)

A U.S. Department of Agriculture photographer films a feature about beef production. The steer does not seem to be impressed.

the largest publishers in the United States, and a great many of its books and pamphlets are illustrated with photographs.

Another large employer of photographers is the National Park Service, which has a huge photographic operation at its many-acre reproduction facility at Harpers Ferry in Virginia. Here, still and motion picture cameramen and women work on everything from photoprints to documentary films. In addition, many field photographers are employed by the Park Service.

Occasionally the government will announce openings for apprentice photographers. Announcements are posted in post offices and local Civil

Service offices, and if you write to them they will notify you. Those hired will receive training in photography while being paid for their work.

Specialized training, especially at the college level, will make it possible for you to qualify for higher-level government photographic jobs. Preparation and updating of maps requires aerial photographers; there are departments of medical photography in many veterans' and other government hospitals; varied types of government research from historical to highly scientific need photographers with specialized training.

For More Information

For information about openings for photographers with the federal government, visit or write to the civil service office that covers the place where you live. (See pages 109–116.)

Federal jobs as photographers are often lifetime positions with pension, health plan, and other benefits. Starting salaries for those with some experience run about $12,000 a year; after some years on the job, the salary may raise to slightly over $20,000 a year.

8 / Undersea Photography

One of the more exciting fields of photography is undersea photography, which combines deep-sea diving and photography. Obviously there is some risk involved in this work, and these diver-photographers are among the highest paid in the field. However, the amount of work available is rather limited, and there is often competition for jobs among the rather small number of qualified persons, which includes some women. A number of those working in the deep waters are former Navy divers who learned the skills while in uniform.

One feature of the job is that there are frequent calls for work in all parts of the world.

In the United States, there are a number of diving schools on both the east and west coasts which teach photography as part of their general courses. However, the Brooks Institute of Photographic Art and Science specializes in training undersea photographers, and we will describe their training program.

They describe their place of training as their campuses in Santa Barbara, California, and the Pacific Ocean.

First, of course, those who might consider this work must pass a thorough medical examination, to discover if they are capable of undergoing the strains of deep-sea diving.

Swim Test

During the first day, the applicant is given the following test in a swimming pool. The test must be passed in order to participate in the program:

1) Swim 1,000 feet—12 minutes.

2) Swim 150 feet underwater—surfacing four times.

3) Swim 75 feet underwater.

4) Tread water—15 minutes.

5) Float 15 minutes.

6) Retrieve 10 pounds of weight from 10-foot depth.

7) Rescue a struggling person.

A diver takes an underwater camera down for a session of picture taking off the coast of Key West, Florida.

(U.S. Navy photo)

(U.S. Navy photo)

This picture shows the undersea photographer's gear: air tanks, breathing tube, goggles, fins, camera, and light.

Diving Equipment

The student must supply all diving equipment, or may rent equipment from the school for the duration of the course.

Required equipment: Wet suit and weight belt, tank, regulator, mask, fins, boots, snorkel, buoyancy compensator. Each student must have his own depth gauge.

Here are the course descriptions:

Undersea Technology Courses

UNDERSEA TECHNOLOGY I

The Curriculum

Undersea I is the beginning class in underwater photography. The first portion of the program is devoted to a (SCUBA) diving training program.

Undersea Photography

For those students who are certified and pass the entrance swim test and written SCUBA exam, their underwater photographic training begins immediately. Undersea I begins with the very basics of underwater photography and will continue to the advanced phase. A research project and paper will also be required in addition to weekly assignments in underwater photography.

Diver Training (SCUBA)

Underwater Photographic Science

- Underwater sensitometry
- Underwater optics
- Film sensitivity and exposure control

Underwater Lighting

- Electronic flash
- Flash bulbs
- Daylight

Underwater Composition and Direction

- Camera equipment and operation
- Camera maintenance
- Laboratory procedures

Underwater Color Photography

- Science of color
- Color harmony
- Presentation of color photographs

UNDERSEA TECHNOLOGY II

Undersea II is an extension of Undersea I, with more emphasis on underwater photographic problems in the still area, motion picture production (primarily camera techniques) and underwater television, video tape systems.

Motion Picture Productions

Cameras and their operation
Basic camera techniques
Development of story
Script writing for underwater films
Production preparation

Motion Picture Underwater Lighting

Daylight
Incandescent
Multi-units

Underwater Television, Video Tape Systems

Operation and methods of use

Still Photography

Multiple lighting units
Multi-media slide presentations

UNDERSEA TECHNOLOGY III

Undersea III is designed to fulfill the needs of the student who wishes an in-depth study in underwater photography.

During the first week the student will be required to research and submit five projects which he or she wants to undertake and finish during the course. The instructor will choose one or two, depending on involvement of the projects.

In addition to these, lectures and assignments will be given in the following areas of offshore photography:

Industrial
Scientific
Illustrative

9 / Photographers in Uniform

Earlier in the book, you read that one way to learn photography is by enlisting in the armed forces and requesting assignment as a photographer.

One Way to Learn Photography

Army photographers are trained with the U.S. Air Force at Lowry Technical Training Center, Denver, Colorado. Soldiers who enlist for photography go there after their basic training. They have the choice of still or motion picture photography. After graduation, they can expect worldwide assignments performing primarily general support photography for a variety of Army customers.

Photo requirements include medical, research and development, combat operations, criminal investigation, and photojournalism.

The Army Program

The Army recently initiated a photojournalism program that offers intermediate-level training in photojournalism at the Defense Information School, Fort Benjamin Harrison, Indiana. The course is open to Army photographers and journalists and lasts seven weeks.

Entry pay for a single recruit is now $397.50. If married, he or she is additionally entitled to a quarters allowance of $142.50. After about three years, a photographer could expect to advance to Specialist 4, which pays $534.90 with a quarters allowance, if married, of $163.50.

(U.S. Navy photo)

These Navy recruits are in "self-paced training" at the Navy Photographic School in Pensacola, Florida. One is using an exposure meter to prepare to shoot an assignment on a Graphic View Camera; the other is checking the image on her view-finder before taking a photo.

(U.S. Navy photo)

The Army's standard small-format camera is the Canon F-1 which is in a kit consisting of a Haliburton case, electronic flash, filters, cable release, a gadget bag, angle finder, and 35 mm, 50 mm, and 135 mm lenses.

In the Navy

"Photographer's Mates" are the U.S. Navy's professional photographers.

These men and women operate different kinds of cameras on a variety of assignments. They cover news events and take pictures for release to Navy

These servicemen are working on a training film in real jungle conditions at Subic Bay in the Philippines. The photographer in the center is using an exposure meter to determine the right exposure for filming in these conditions.

(*U.S. Navy photo*)

or civilian publications, or for use in historical documents. Their work may include portrait photography, photographic copying, aerial photography for mapmaking or reconnaissance, and the preparation of training and other types of motion pictures. They are also responsible for camera maintenance and repair as well as film processing.

The duties of Photographer's Mates:

Operate and maintain and repair various types of cameras for a variety of uses.

Perform duties as members of flight crews.

Develop motion picture film and microfilm prints.

Take news photographs.

Operate laboratory and darkroom equipment for film processing.

Mix photographic chemicals and solutions.

Prepare audio-visual presentations.

Operate TV cameras and produce TV features.

Navy Requirements

In assignment of personnel to photographic training, the Navy tries to choose those who meet these requirements (which also seem to apply to civilian photographers):

Must be able to relate to people in a very creative and understanding way. Curiosity, a good memory, good speaking and writing ability, the ability to do detail work, keep records, and perform repetitive tasks are all very important qualifications for this rating. Good color vision is required. Teamwork, arithmetic ability, and a degree of manual dexterity and physical strength are also helpful.

(U.S. Navy photo)

Photographer's Mates in the Navy learn to handle the most complicated photographic equipment. Here, a P.M. is checking a Vigilante Attack Aircraft camera system aboard an attack aircraft carrier.

Those selected for training are sent to the Class "A" technical school at Pensacola, Florida, for a ten- or eleven-week course in basic photography.

Then they may be assigned to any kind of ship, shore station, Navy photo center, naval air station, or other naval activity. Some will learn deep-water photography at a Navy diving school.

The Navy estimates that during a twenty-year hitch a Navy photographer will spend about forty to fifty percent of the time assigned to fleet units, fifty to sixty percent at shore stations.

(U.S. Navy photo)

Hanging from a sky hook? Not quite. This Navy photographer is being hoisted from the water to a tower during a simulated helicopter pickup. He's taking pictures from an air crew trainee's point of view in what the Navy calls "deep water environmental survival training."

Working Conditions

Photographer's Mates work wherever their assignments take them–indoors, outdoors, in all kinds of climate and weather. While processing film, they work indoors in comfortable temperatures. The actual work they perform is mostly mental, but getting into position to take a photograph can involve strenuous, even hazardous effort.

Although there are more than 2,500 Navy photographers, there are many applicants for every opening and those who make it are highly qualified.

When they leave the Navy, the photographers are qualified for jobs as developers, aerial photographers, and commercial photographers.

For More Information

To learn more about opportunities for photographers in the armed forces, you can phone or visit the recruiting station in your area. You will find it listed in the white pages of the telephone directory under "United States Government–Army and Navy Recruiting Stations." Also, many magazines carry advertisements telling where to call or write for this information.

10 / Biological Photography

An Arm of Science

Biological photographers say that theirs is the largest field of scientific photography, and that it is growing at a good pace.

If you are science-minded, a career in scientific photography is worth your consideration.

Photography is frequently used as a method of scientific recording. Entomologists carry cameras on their field trips to make photographic recording of insects, pathologists photograph images seen in their microscopes, and astronauts take pictures of rocks on the moon.

But photography is not restricted to recording of things or events seen by the human eye. Using ultraviolet or infrared radiation, the photographer can record things that the human eye cannot see because it is not sensitive to these forms of radiant energy.

By means of high-speed cinematography it is possible to photograph events that occur too fast for the eye to follow. When the film of these events is projected slower than it was photographed, their images can be easily analyzed and measured.

On the other hand, some events take place much too slowly to be observed. Growth of a colony of bacteria may take several hours or days; plants may require weeks or months, but time-lapse pho-

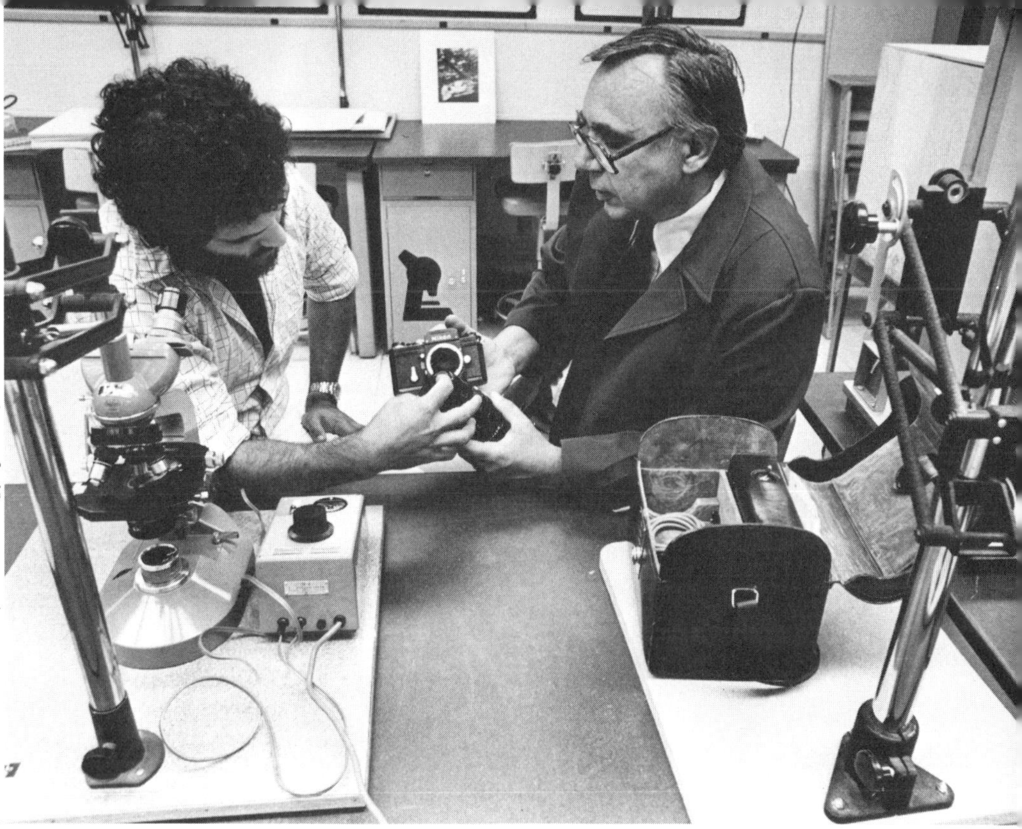
(Rochester Institute of Technology photo)

Here, a Rochester Institute of Technology student gets some instruction on the use of the long lens for biomedical photography. This is part of the National Technical Institute program for the deaf student.

tography speeds up their growth on the screen so that it may be easily observed.

To be useful for scientific purposes, photography must be extremely precise. To avoid errors, the scientific photographer must have a thorough knowledge of optics, light theory, and of photosensitive materials, as well as adequate knowledge of the subject matter he or she is recording. For these photographers, photography is a science in its own right. If you study the pages of a magazine like *Science, Natural History, Scientific American,*

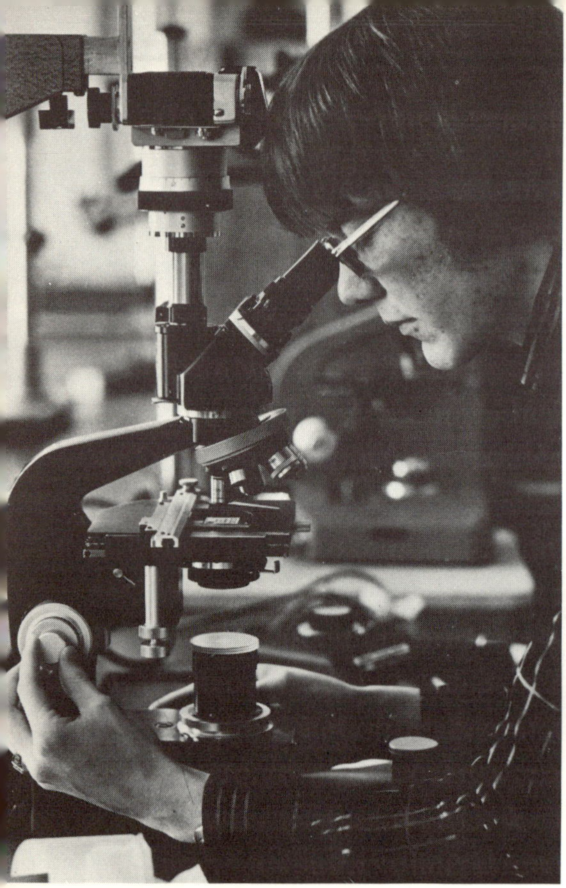

(Rochester Institute of Technology photo)

Micro-photography is a procedure which combines the use of the magnifying microscope and the camera. Here, an R.I.T. student learns this technique.

or *The Smithsonian,* you will see examples of the work of scientific photographers.

The difference between scientific and commercial photography is basic. The scientific uses all available skill and knowledge to reproduce everything as accurately as possible. The commercial photographer, for whom photography is a form of art, will use all possible ingenuity to show objects in the most appealing way, no matter how artificial or even distorted they may appear.

A Demanding Job

Modern methods and equipment used in scientific photography today are so complex that casual on-the-job training is no longer adequate. The biological photographer is now expected to use a large variety of still and motion picture cameras and other equipment to document an enormous variety of subjects. In heart transplant operations, in addition to photographic skills the photographer must be able to work in the operating room without endangering the patient or interfering with the medical team. In the filming of chromosomes in a dividing cell through a high-power microscope, the photographer must know his camera work as well as having a thorough knowledge of microscopy. The knowledge and experience demanded of a scientific photographer can only be acquired through professional training followed by several years of practical work.

The Educational Background

A number of schools and colleges offer courses leading to science degrees in biological photography. Many working biological photographers are alumni of the Rochester Institute of Technology, where a two-year course leading to an associate degree in biomedical photography and a four-year course leading to a bachelor's degree are offered.

Undergraduate and postgraduate courses in this field are offered by several institutions where a master's degree in biomedical communications can be earned. These colleges and universities are listed in the Kodak directory *A Survey of Motion Picture, Still Photography, and Graphic Arts Instruction,* available from the Eastman Kodak Company, Rochester, N.Y. 14650.

The following description of a course in medical and scientific photography, which requires the earlier completion of a basic course in photogra-

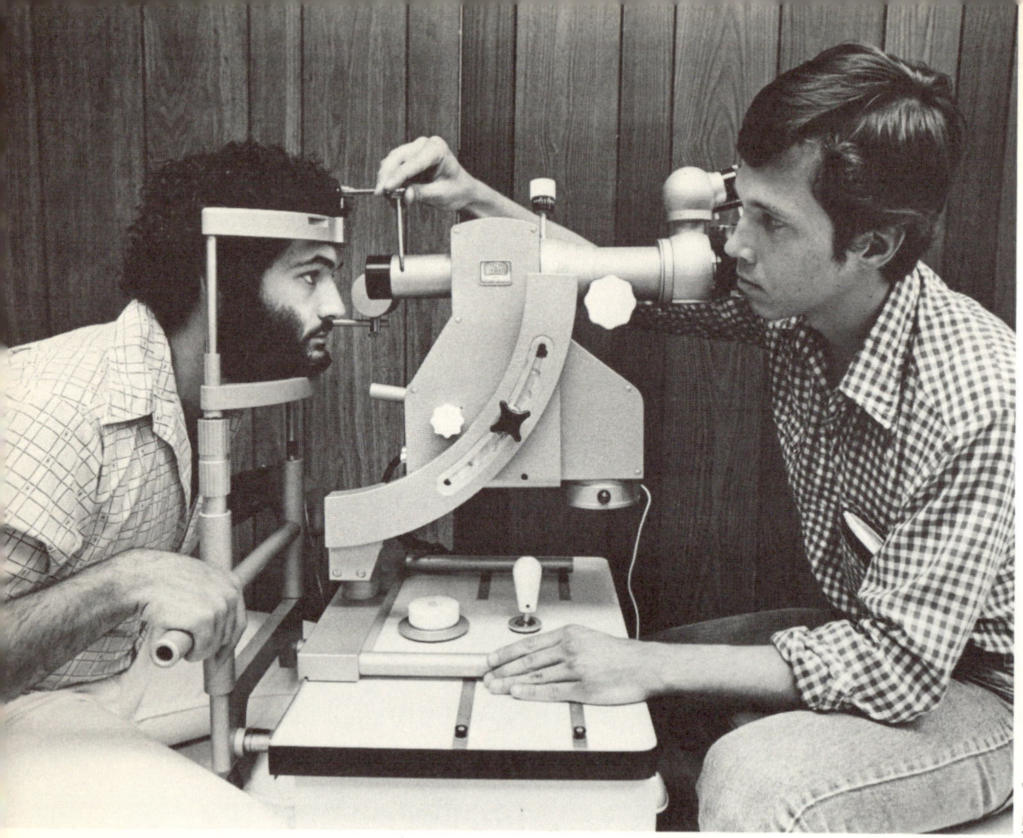

(Rochester Institute of Technology photo)

The fundus camera being used by these students is a special type that takes pictures of the interior of the eye. This enables eye doctors, ophthalmologists, to keep track of changing conditions in a patient's eyes, and gives them more time to study eye conditions than they could have without the photographs.

phy, gives you an idea of the wide range of knowledge required:

A Course in Medical and Scientific Photography

MEDICAL AND SCIENTIFIC PHOTOGRAPHY 150 Hours

This course is designed to train you in the specialized techniques of bio-medical photography. Combining school and studio work with location shooting in the hospital and operating room, the course provides instruction in those areas required by physicians, medical centers, and research institutions.

Occupational Objective: Self-employment; entry employment as a medical or scientific photographer.

Prerequisites: A basic course in still photography or equivalent training or field experience. The following topics are covered:

Copying and Printing for the Educational and Presentation Media
Basic Principles of Copying; Copying Radiographs; 35 mm Direct and Reversal Copying; Intermediate Negatives to Positive Transparencies; Copying of Electrocardiograms, Electroencephalograms, and Cardiovectors; Special Films; Photography of Electrophoresis and Chromatography; Films and Filters; Line Copies; Drawings; Charts; Graphs; Continuous Tones; Copying Color Transparencies; Lantern Slides; Diazo Printing; Color Guide and Transparex Printing; Color and Black-and white Projection Slide Production.

Patient Photography
Plastic Surgery; Standard Positions; Orthopedic Photography; Obstetrics; Pediatrics; Oral and Dental Photography; Photography of Dermatological Subjects; Burns, Breasts, External Genitalia and Varicosities; Opthalmology; Operating Room

Photography; Inpatient Photography; Public Relations.

Photomicrography, Specimen Photography, and Microbiology Photography
Photomicrography; Compound Microscopes; Microbiology; Photography; Cultures; Diffusion Discs; Electrophoresis Slide Plates; Photography of Gross Specimens; Macrophotography.

To round out professional training, internship programs have been established at some biomedical establishments. The biological photographer is now a highly skilled member of the scientific team. He or she supports research scientists in their work, helps the medical practitioner to deliver better health care, and helps the educator to provide better training for more students.

For More Information

The Biological Photographic Association was founded at Yale in 1931, and now has well over 1,000 members in the United States and Canada.

The BPA maintains a board of registry so that qualified biological photographers can have their knowledge and experience confirmed by passing required examinations, and becoming certified as registered biological photographers.

For further information regarding the profession, its educational opportunities, or the Association, contact:

Executive Secretary
Biological Photographic Association
Stanley J. McComb, RBP
P.O. Box 1057, Rochester, Minnesota 55901

Other useful sources of information are:

American Society of Photogrammetry
105 North Virginia Avenue
Falls Church, Virginia 22046

Eastman Kodak Company
Department 761 C
Rochester, New York 14650

National Microfilm Association
8728 Colesville Road, Suite 1101
Silver Spring, Maryland 20910

Society of Photographic Scientists and Engineers
1330 Massachusetts Avenue, N.W.
Washington, D.C. 20005

Society of Photo-Optical Instrumentation Engineers
338 Tejon Place
Palos Verdes Estates, California 90274

Appendix

Civil Service Commission Offices

These are the Civil Service Offices where you can get information about opportunities for photographers in the Federal Government:

State and city	*Area served*
WASHINGTON, D.C. 20415 Civil Service Commission Bldg. 1900 E. St. NW.	District of Columbia; Charles, Montgomery, and Prince Georges counties, Md.; Arlington, Fairfax, Prince William, King George, Stafford, and Loudoun counties, Va.; Alexandria, Falls Church, and Fairfax, Va.; and overseas areas except Western Pacific area
ALABAMA Huntsville 35801 Southerland Bldg. 806 Governors Dr. SW.	Northern Alabama
Mobile 36602 First National Bank Bldg. 107 St. Francis St.	Southern Alabama (excluding Russell county) and Florida counties west of Apalachicola River (See Macon, Ga.)
ALASKA Anchorage 99051 Hill Bldg., 632 6th Ave.	Alaska
Fairbanks 99701 Fort Wainwright	Subsidiary to Anchorage
ARIZONA Phoenix 85003 Balke Bldg. 44 W. Adams St.	Arizona (except Navajo-Hopi Indian Reservations) (See Albuquerque, New Mex.)
ARKANSAS Little Rock 72203 923 W. Fourth St.	Arkansas (except Crittenden and Miller counties) (See Memphis, Tenn., and Dallas, Tex.)
CALIFORNIA Los Angeles 90014 Eastern Columbia Bldg. 851 S. Broadway	Kern, Los Angeles, Orange, San Luis Obispo, Santa Barbara, and Ventura counties

State and city	*Area served*
Long Beach 90813 1340 Pine Ave.	Subsidiary to Los Angeles
Santa Maria 93454 Rm. 207 Post Office Bldg. 120 W. Cypress St.	Subsidiary to Los Angeles
Sacramento 95814 650 Capitol Mall, Rm. 4210	California (except Lassen county) (See Reno, Nevada)
San Bernardino 92401 380 W. Court St	Riverside and San Bernardino counties
San Diego 92101 1400 5th Ave., Suite 100	San Diego and Imperial counties
San Francisco 94102 450 Golden Gate Ave. Box 36122	San Francisco area and Central Western California
COLORADO Denver 80202 Rm. 203, Post Office Bldg. 18th and Stout Streets	Colorado
CONNECTICUT Hartford 06103 Rm. 716, Federal Bldg. 450 Main St.	Connecticut and Berkshire, Franklin, Hampden, and Hampshire counties, Mass.
DELAWARE Wilmington 19801 Post Office and Court-house 11th and King Sts.	Delaware
FLORIDA Orlando 32803 3101 Maguire Blvd.	Florida east of Apalachicola River (See Mobile, Ala.)
GEORGIA Atlanta 30303 275 Peachtree St. NE.	Northern Georgia (except Walker county) (See Memphis, Tenn.)

State and city	*Area served*
Macon 31201 Federal Bldg. 451 College St.	Southern Georgia; Russell county, Ala.; and Aiken county, S.C.
HAWAII Honolulu 96813 Federal Bldg.	Hawaii and Western Pacific area
IDAHO Boise 83702 Rm. 663, Fed. Bldg. U.S. Courthouse 550 W. Fort St.	Idaho
ILLINOIS Chicago 60604 Rm. 1322 219 S. Dearborn St.	Illinois (except Madison and St. Clair counties) and Scott county, Iowa (See St. Louis, Mo.)
Great Lakes 60088 Bldg. 3400, Electronics Supply Office	Subsidiary to Chicago
Rock Island 61201 Bldg. 103 Rock Island Arsenal	Subsidiary to Chicago
INDIANA Indianapolis 46204 Rm. 102 36 S. Pennsylvania St.	Indiana (except Clark, Dearborn, and Floyd counties) and Henderson county, Ky. (See Louisville, Ky., and Dayton, Ohio)
IOWA Des Moines 50309 191 Federal Bldg. 210 Walnut St.	Iowa (except Scott and Pottawattamie counties) (See Omaha, Nebr., and Chicago, Ill.)
KANSAS Wichita 67202 Rm. 101, One-Twenty Bldg. 120 So. Market St.	Kansas (except Johnson, Leavenworth, and Wyandotte counties) (See Kansas City, Mo.)
KENTUCKY Louisville 40202 Rm. 167, Federal Bldg. 600 Federal Plaza	Kentucky (except Boone, Boyd, Campbell, Christian, Henderson, and Kenton counties) and Clark and Floyd counties, Ind. (See Dayton, Ohio, Charleston, W. Va., and Memphis, Tenn.)

State and city	*Area served*
LOUISIANA New Orleans 70130 Federal Building South 600 South St.	Louisiana
MAINE Augusta 04330 Federal Bldg.	Maine
MARYLAND Baltimore 21201 Federal Office Bldg. Lombard St. and Hopkins Pl.	Maryland (except Montgomery, Prince Georges, and Charles counties) (See Washington, D.C.)
MASSACHUSETTS Boston 02109 Post Office and Courthouse Bldg. Room 1004	Boston area (Essex, Norfolk, Middlesex, Plymouth, Suffolk, and Worcester counties) (See Hartford, Conn., and Providence, R.I.)
MICHIGAN Detroit 48226 Lobby, 1st Floor 144 W. Lafayette St.	Michigan
MINNESOTA Twin Cities 55111 Rm. 196, Federal Bldg. Ft. Snelling	Minnesota (except Clay county) and Douglas county, Wis. (See Fargo, N. Dak.)
MISSISSIPPI Jackson 39201 802 N. State St.	Mississippi
MISSOURI Kansas City 64106 Federal Bldg., Rm. 129 601 E. 12th St.	Western Missouri and Johnson, Leavenworth, and Wyandotte counties, Kans.
St. Louis 63103 Federal Bldg., Rm. 1712 1520 Market St.	Eastern Missouri and Madison and St. Clair counties, Ill.

State and city	*Area served*
MONTANA Helena 59601 I.B.M. Bldg. 130 Neill Ave.	Montana
NEBRASKA Omaha 68102 Courthouse and Post Office Bldg., Rm. 1014 215 N. 17th St.	Nebraska and Pottawattamie county, Iowa
NEVADA Reno 89502 Fed. Bldg., Room 1139 300 Booth St.	Nevada and Lassen County, Calif.
Las Vegas 89101 300 Las Vegas Blvd. S.	Subsidiary to Reno
NEW HAMPSHIRE Portsmouth 03803 Federal Bldg.-U.S. Post Office Daniel and Penhallow Sts.	New Hampshire (except Hanover and Lebanon, N.H., areas) (See Burlington, Vt.)
NEW JERSEY Newark 07102 Federal Bldg. 970 Broad St.	New Jersey (except Camden county) (See Philadelphia, Pa.)
NEW MEXICO Albuquerque 87101 Federal Bldg. 421 Gold Ave. S.W.	New Mexico (except Dona Ana and Otero counties) and Navajo-Hopi Indian Reservations in Arizona (See El Paso, Texas, and Phoenix, Ariz.)
NEW YORK New York 10007 Federal Bldg. 26 Federal Plaza	New York City; Long Island; and Rockland, Westchester, Orange, Putnam, and Dutchess counties

State and city	*Area served*
Syracuse 13202 O'Donnell Bldg. 301 Erie Blvd. W.	Northern New York
NORTH CAROLINA Raleigh 27611 310 New Bern Ave. Fed. Office Bldg.	North Carolina
NORTH DAKOTA Fargo 58102 Rm. 200, Federal Bldg. and Post Office 657 Second Ave.	North Dakota and Clay county, Minn.
OHIO Cleveland 44199 New Federal Bldg. 1240 E. 9th St.	Northern Ohio
Dayton 45402 Knott Bldg. 21 E. 4th St.	Southern Ohio (excluding Belmont, Jefferson, and Lawrence counties) and Dearborn county, Ind., and Boone, Campbell, and Kenton counties, Ky. (See Charleston, W. Va.)
Cincinnati 45202 Rm. 1523 Federal Office Bldg. 550 Main St.	Subsidiary to Dayton
OKLAHOMA Oklahoma City 73102 210 NW. 6th St.	Oklahoma
OREGON Portland 97204 319 SW. Pine St.	Oregon and Clark counties, Wash.
PENNSYLVANIA Philadelphia 19102 128 N. Broad St.	Eastern Pennsylvania and Camden county, N.J.
Pittsburgh 15222 Federal Bldg. 1000 Liberty Ave.	Central and Western Pennsylvania

State and city	*Area served*
PUERTO RICO Hato Rey 00917 Pan Am Bldg. 255 Ponce de Leon Ave.	Puerto Rico and Virgin Islands
RHODE ISLAND Providence 02903 Federal Bldg. and Post Office Kennedy Plaza	Rhode Island and Barnstable, Bristol, Dukes, and Nantucket counties, Mass.
SOUTH CAROLINA Charleston 29403 Federal Office Bldg. 334 Meeting St.	South Carolina (except Aiken county) (See Macon, Ga.)
SOUTH DAKOTA Rapid City 57701 Dusek Bldg., 919 Main St. Rm. 118	South Dakota
TENNESSEE Memphis 38103 Federal Office Bldg. 167 N. Main St.	Tennessee and Crittenden county, Ark., Christian county, Ky., and Walker county, Ga.
TEXAS Dallas 75202 Rm. 103 1114 Commerce St.	Northern Texas and Miller county, Ark.
Fort Worth 76102 819 Taylor St.	Subsidiary to Dallas
El Paso 79901 El Paso National Bank Bldg. 411 N. Stanton St.	Western Texas and Dona Ana and Otero counties, N. Mex.
Houston 77002 702 Caroline St.	Gulf Coast
Corpus Christi 78401 Downtown Postal Bldg. 701 N. Upper Bdwy.	Subsidiary to Houston

State and city	*Area served*
San Antonio 78205 Post Office and Courthouse Bldg. 615 E. Houston St.	South Central Texas
UTAH Salt Lake City 84111 Federal Bldg. Annex 135 S. State St.	Utah
VERMONT Burlington 05401 Federal Bldg. Elmwood Ave. and Pearl St.	Vermont and Hanover and Lebanon, N.H., areas
VIRGIN ISLANDS	(See Puerto Rico)
VIRGINIA Norfolk 23510 Rotunda Bldg. 415 St. Paul Blvd.	Virginia (except Arlington, Fairfax, Stafford, Prince William, King George, and Loudoun counties, and Alexandria, Falls Church, and Fairfax) (See Washington, D.C.)
WASHINGTON Seattle 98104 Federal Office Bldg. 1st Ave. and Madison St.	Washington (except Clark county) (See Portland, Oreg.)
Bremerton 98314 511 Burwell St.	Subsidiary to Seattle
WEST VIRGINIA Charleston 25301 Federal Bldg. 500 Quarrier St.	West Virginia and Belmont, Jefferson, and Lawrence counties, Ohio, and Boyd county, Ky.
WISCONSIN Milwaukee 53203 Rm. 215 161 W. Wisconsin Ave.	Wisconsin (except Douglas county) (See Twin Cities, Minn.)
WYOMING Cheyenne 82001 Rm. 108 1805 Capitol Ave.	Wyoming

Glossary for Photographers

Accelerators: Chemicals having the property of speeding up the activity of a photographic solution.

Acetate Base: Film base made of cellulose acetate.

Acetic Acid: A clear, colorless liquid used in a variety of photographic solutions.

Achromatic: Without color.

Actinic Light: Any light that will affect a photographic emulsion.

Affinity: The tendency for one chemical to react with another.

Agitation: The movement of solution, film, or paper, during processing, to ensure thorough and even chemical action.

Alkali: The opposite of acid: used as accelerator in developers.

American Standards Association (ASA): An organization whose major purpose is to gather, correlate, and standardize information about photographic material, processes, and equipment.

Anastigmatic lens: A lens corrected for astigmatism.

Angle–Camera: Position of the camera relative to the subject.

Angle of View (of a lens): The angular coverage a lens produces on a film.

Angular Field (of a lens): The entire area covered by the lens.

Anhydrous: A chemical term indicating dry, or without water.

Antihalation Backing: A backing on most photographic films, which absorbs light after it has passed through the emulsion, preventing the light from reflecting into the emulsion and creating a "halation."

Aperture: The opening in a diaphragm of a lens through which light passes. In a motion picture camera or projector, it is the opening which outlines a frame in the film track.

Apochromatic Lens: A lens corrected to a very high degree for all colors.

ASA Exposure Index: A numerical value assigned to film by ASA to indicate its speed and for use in computing correct exposure.

Astigmatism: A lens aberration which prevents a lens from focusing horizontal and vertical lines sharply at the same time.

Base, Film: The material upon which the light-sensitive photographic emulsion is coated.

Blow-Up: To enlarge a photograph; a big enlargement.

Bulb: One of the settings on a camera shutter speed control. Shutter remains open as long as the trip mechanism is depressed.

Celsius: The temperature scale using 0° as the

freezing point of water, and 100° as the boiling point of water. Replaces the Fahrenheit scale.

Cinematography: Motion picture photography.

Closeup: A scene, in motion pictures, filmed at very close range to show intimate detail. In still photography, any photograph made with a very short camera-to-subject distance.

Continuity: In motion pictures, the logical connection of scenes and sequences to tell a story intelligently.

Contrast: The difference in tones from the lightest to the darkest areas of negatives and positives.

Depth of Field: The depth of field of a lens is that area between the nearest point and the farthest point in acceptably sharp focus.

Emulsion: A light-sensitive coating for photographic films and papers, consisting of silver salts suspended in gelatin.

Fan: In aerial photography, two or more cameras arranged so that their images overlap to give continuous coverage from horizon to horizon.

Flat: Lack of contrast.

Focus: 1. To adjust the distance between lens and film for maximum image sharpness. 2. The point at which converging rays of light, focused by a lens, cross.

Halation: A fog or halo around brilliantly lighted objects, due to light which passed completely through the emulsion and is reflected into the emulsion.

Hertz: The term used to replace "cycles per second."

Hypo: The common name for sodium thiosulfate; also used by photographers when speaking of the complete fixing bath.

Image: The representation of an object or scene formed by optical or chemical means.

Infinity: Unlimited extent of space; in practical photography, objects at a distance of 500 feet or more are considered to be at infinity.

Latent Image: The image recorded on a light-sensitive emulsion by light that remained invisible until developed.

Lens Shade or *Lens Hood:* An attachment fastened to the lens to prevent the direct rays of a light source from striking the lens surface.

Long Shot: In motion pictures, a scene filmed at a considerable distance.

Monochromatic: Having only one color.

Mosaic: An assemblage of overlapping aerial photographs whose edges have been matched to form a continuous photographic map.

Negative: A photographic image in which the tones of the subject have been recorded in reverse.

Oblique: Mainly in aerial photography, a photograph taken with the camera aimed anywhere from the horizon to a line almost perpendicular to the ground.

Opacity: Light-stopping ability.

Opal Glass: A translucent glass having a milky or

opalescent appearance, used to diffuse light.

Opaque: The property of a substance that will not transmit light. Also, a paint-like substance applied to negatives to block the passage of light through certain areas.

Pan: In camera techniques, the moving of the camera while shooting. In films, it describes a type of emulsion, "panchromatic," which is sensitive to all colors of the visible spectrum.

Photogrammetry: The science of mapping and surveying photographically.

Photomacrography: Small objects photographed at greater than life size by the use of long bellows and short focal length cameras.

Pinholes: Tiny transparent spots on a negative or positive image.

Polarized Light: Light vibrating in one direction.

Primary Colors: Three colors of light–red, blue, and green–which when mixed in equal amounts produce white light.

Reducing Agent: Any chemical that reduces (develops) silver salts in emulsion to metallic silver.

Refraction: The bending of light as it enters or leaves transparent mediums of different densities.

Resolving Power or *Resolution:* The ability of a lens to separate closely spaced details of an object.

Sharp: Term used to denote the distinctness of detail in a photograph or the focused image on the ground glass of a camera.

Shutter: A device installed in front, behind, or between the elements of a lens, or at the focal point of the camera, to control the length of exposure.

Stock Solution: A concentrated solution, which, when diluted with water, makes a working solution.

Stop Bath: A weak acid solution used immediately after developing and before fixing to stop the action of the developer.

Thin: As applied to negatives; weak, lacking in detail in highlights and shadows. (Underexposed or underdeveloped.)

Time Lapse Photography: A motion picture, or series of slides or prints, that shows in a few minutes or seconds events that take hours or even days to occur; accomplished by exposing single frames or film shots at fixed intervals.

Transparency: A positive image on a transparent base, which may be projected.

Washed Out: The term used to describe a print lacking in highlight detail.

Wetting Agent: A substance added to water to improve its wetting characteristics. It reduces the surface tension of the water, thereby allowing it to drain evenly and rapidly from film without leaving spots.

Working Solution: A solution ready for use without dilution.

Work Print: In motion pictures, the print on which all editing is done.

Bibliography

Books

Edna Bennett, *Careers in Photography.* Amphoto Publishers, 750 Zeckendorf Boulevard, Garden City, New York 11530.

Jacob Deschin, *Photography in Your Future.* Macmillan Publishing Company, 866 Third Avenue, New York, N.Y. 10022.

Rodney Fox and Robert Kerns, *Creative News Photography.* Iowa State University Press, Press Building, Ames, Iowa 50010.

Stan Holden, *20 Ways to Make Money in Photography.* Amphoto.

Lou Jacobs, Jr., *Free Lance Magazine Photography.* Amphoto.

———, *Instant Photography.* Lothrop, Lee & Shepard Company, 105 Madison Avenue, New York, N.Y. 10016.

Victor Keppler, *Your Future in Photography.* Richards Rosen Press, 29 East 21st Street, New York, N.Y. 10003.

Floyd McCall and Robert B. Rhode, *Press Photography.* Macmillan.

Roy Pinney, *Careers with a Camera.* J. B. Lippincott Company, 521 Fifth Ave., New York, N.Y. 10017.

Lou and Zena Shumsky, *Shutterbug.* Thomas Y. Crowell Company, 521 Fifth Ave., New York, N.Y. 10017.

Pamphlets

Careers for You. Society of Motion Picture and Television Engineers, 862 Scarsdale Ave., Scarsdale, N.Y. 10583.

Careers in Motion Picture Production (C-3-87). Eastman Kodak Company Photo Information, Department 841, 343 State Street, Rochester, N.Y. 14650.

To obtain the following, first write for price list:

Chronicle Occupational Briefs. Chronicle Guidance Publications, Inc., Moravia, N.Y. 13188.
No. 12—Photographers
No. 310—Photographic Darkroom Occupations

Occupational Briefs. Science Research Associates, Inc., 259 East Erie Street, Chicago, Ill. 60611.

05990035	Commercial and Industrial Photographers
05990329	Film Editors
05990257	Motion Picture Producers
05990264	Press Photographers

Job Fact Sheet. Council for Career Planning, 541 Madison Ave., New York, N.Y. 10022
No. 29—Job Fact Sheet: Photography

Starting and Managing a Small Retail Camera Store (Cat. SBA 1.15:17; S/N 4500-0063). Public Documents Department, U.S. Government Printing Office, Washington, D.C. 20402. (This is out of print, but many libraries have copies.)

Photographers–Photographic Laboratory Workers. Occupational Outlook Bulletin No. 116, Superintendent of Documents, U.S. Government Printing Office, Washington, D.C. 20402.

Biological Photography—A Challenging Profession. Free from Biological Photographic Association, Inc., P.O. Box 1057, Rochester, Minn. 55901.

Careers in Photography. Free from Germain School of Photography, 225 Broadway, New York, N.Y. 10017.

Focus on Your Future. Free from Professional Photographers of America, Inc., 1090 Executive Way, Oak Leaf Commons, Des Plaines, Ill. 60018.

Catalog of Photographic Books. Free from American Photographic Book Publishing Company, Inc., Garden City, N.Y., 11530.

Photography–Merit Badge Pamphlet. Boy Scouts of America, North Brunswick, N.J. 08902.

Photography Manual. Girl Scouts of America, 830 Third Ave., New York, N.Y. 10022.

Photography Training Manuals

If you want to study photography on your own, about the best material available is in two manuals used by the U.S. Navy to train photographers. You can get them by sending a check to: Superintendent of Documents, Government Printing Office, Washington, D.C. 20402. They are:

Photographer's Mate 1 and C	$5.80
Stock No. 008-047-00179-7	
Photographer's Mate 3 and 2	$9.00
Stock No. 008-047-00146-1	

Magazines

Industrial Photography. 750 Third Avenue, New York, N.Y. 10017.

Petersen's Photographic Magazine. 8490 Sunset Boulevard, Los Angeles, Calif. 90069.

Professional Photographer. 1090 Executive Way, Des Plaines, Ill. 60018.

Market Guides

The following market guides are intended to assist free-lance photographers in selling their work. When you come to that stage, you will probably find them most helpful. Meanwhile, they will give you an idea of the many buyers of free-lance photography. Look for these in your local library:

Melissa Milar and William Brohaugh, editors, *Photographer's Market* (annual editions): Writer's Digest, Cincinnati, Ohio. Lists advertising agencies, architectural firms, audiovisual firms, book publishers, and periodicals.

Fred McDarrah, editor, *Photography Market Place:* R. R. Bowker, Co., New York, N.Y. Contains some 5,500 separate listings.

Index

Italics indicate illustration